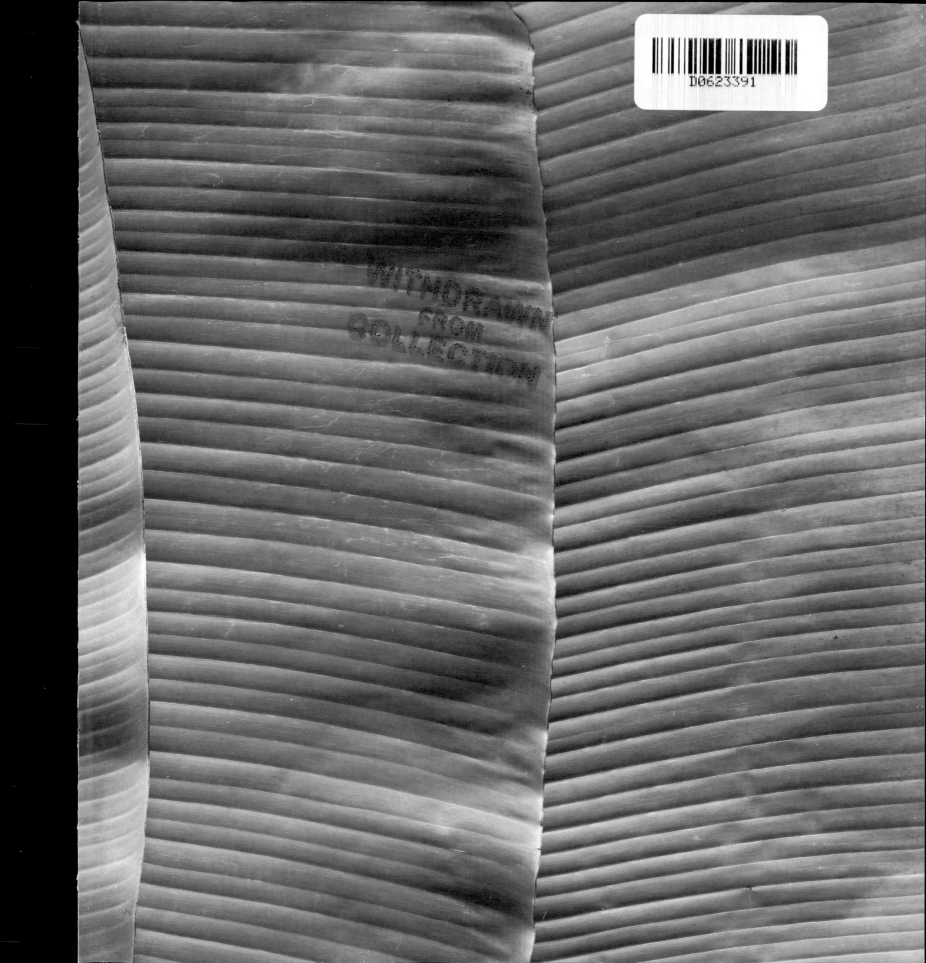

My Feast

with **PETER KURUVITA**

A REMARKABLE JOURNEY
THROUGH ISLAND CUISINE

hardie grant books
MELBOURNE · LONDON

SBS

DEDICATION

This book is dedicated to the millions of people who live their lives simply, surviving day to day, uncertain of where their next dollar or job might be coming from. They are passionate and caring people who, even though they may not have much, would give you the shirts off their backs and their last handfuls of rice if you asked them.

We can learn from these people. Despite their hardships, they demonstrate that a peaceful and simple life can be very fulfilling.

Contents

Beginnings

As a kid growing up in Sri Lanka, food was a very important part of life. You not only knew how good food tasted but you also knew what it was good for. For example, if you were at the market and asked an older person what a certain vegetable was, you would first be told of its Ayurvedic properties, before being told how it should be prepared.

Things changed very dramatically for me in 1975 when we immigrated to Australia. I was eleven years old. Leaving our 250-year-old ancestral home in Dehiwala, Colombo, and all our relatives and comforts, we arrived in a new land, a harsh land where our traditions meant nothing and we were nobody. We arrived not long after the White Australia policy had ended and lived in the then wild western suburbs of Sydney. It was a shock to the system. Add to that a very healthy serve of racism not only towards me but my parents — an Austrian mother and Sri Lankan father — and you had a child who hated the world. I fought it and anyone that dealt it out with vigour. My love of food and hours spent with my grandmother and aunties in their kitchen back in Sri Lanka were suppressed and survival mode kicked in.

Cooking never occurred to me again until my dad said, 'Get out of my car and go and ask for a job'. I was sixteen years and nine months old. School and I did not agree with each other; a fact that did not sit well with my dad, a very proud engineer, who already had one son at university studying science and another on his way to being an engineer and pilot. I was a wayward and rebellious middle son. I was never going to fit the mould of my siblings and finally got my way and left school.

Within a week of leaving school, I was constantly being asked what I wanted to do for work. I really did not know. I was never scared of work and by sixteen I could pull a car to bits and put it back together with my eyes closed.

I had worked with my dad doing all the renovations about our house so I knew the basics of all the trades; building, carpentry, electrical and plumbing, which would serve me well for the rest of my life and save me thousands in dollars, but I did not want to take up any of those trades as a career.

So there I was on the main street of Mortdale, where we then lived in suburban Sydney, looking at my dad who had just ordered me into The Crabapple restaurant to ask for a job.

This was not a random place that Dad chose for me to begin my working career. Part of the deal with my leaving school was that I had to complete my school certificate but to do that I had to complete an elective — and the only options available were cookery or needlework. I was okay with a needle and thread, but there was no way I was going to take up a needlework class. I liked the girls in the cooking class better and opted for cookery instead. I loved it and topped the class. But it didn't yet click that cookery was to be my path.

I got out of the car and looked back at Dad and thought to myself, 'What is he thinking?' As I stepped onto the threshold of the little shop front, my first memory of a restaurant was formed — the smell of a restaurant that has slept for the night, the lingering smell of oil, garlic and seafood still hanging in the air. Those smells are now very familiar and as a restaurant warms up and the chefs start cooking, the smells freshen and life is again breathed back into the building.

I walked in and a healthy looking young chef with a glint in his eye called me into his kitchen. His name was Scott Mylrea and he would become my mentor in many ways. Calm, friendly and knowledgeable, he took me for who I was and taught me the basics of cookery. I started my life in the culinary world that night. I was cooking!

It was like I had rewound five years and was in the loving embrace of my Sri Lankan family, where food was paramount and how you cooked reflected on your whole family.

I was very lucky and am thankful to my dad for forcing me into that restaurant, and to the Mylrea family for taking me in. I was a natural. I picked things up immediately, and had worked my way up to cooking mains in only three months. I was so happy — for the first time in a very long time. I was working hard, had no interaction with anyone from my schooling life and worked anti-social hours. I was in heaven. I had found my passion.

The next few years flew by, but I knew that this job could be my passport to the world. I realised that with a bit of passion and flexibility I could travel anywhere, do anything and achieve any goal I wanted. The recipe was easy: lots of hard work, a little bit of luck, and a tonne of grim determination. None of those attributes were foreign to me.

So I formed my plans — sous chef as soon as possible, head chef as young as I could, executive chef in a five-star hotel, lots of travel, and work in as many countries as I could. But most of all, live a full and exciting life.

That was thirty-three years ago, and I am still having adventures, cooking and travelling ... which takes me to the adventure I want to share with you in this book: my islands journey.

As this book is loosely formed around my two television shows, *My Sri Lanka* and *Island Feast*, I will give you a quick recount of how it all came about. I was approached by a young producer called Henry Motteram who wanted to produce some online video content for the website of our Flying Fish restaurant in Sydney. We talked lots and got to know each other quite well, and then Henry left the company and launched his own production company.

Twenty-three years prior to that, when I was the head chef of a big harbourside restaurant, I met Merrill J Fernando, founder and chairman of Dilmah tea, . Mr Fernando was in Australia to launch his company, Dilmah, and introduce to Australia pure Ceylon tea — unblended, single-estate tea

picked and packed at the source; something that Dilmah still leads the world of tea in. Over the years we kept in touch and I started to get more involved in the Dilmah story and the gastronomical marriage of tea and food. One day I got a message that Dilmah was to run a program called *The Chef and the Tea Maker* in which eight chefs from Australia would be taken to Sri Lanka to be introduced to tea gastronomy. I was asked to assemble the chefs, a photographer and a film crew to record this unique experience. I asked Henry to submit a quote, and his new production company, The Precinct Studios, was awarded the job.

While we were in Sri Lanka, a country still in the grip of a terrible civil war, Henry and I saw the potential to do a television series about the country and its food. All we needed was a show reel and a television station to pick it up. I had just finished my first cookbook, *Serendip - My Sri Lankan Kitchen*, and thought it would be easy. So with show reel and book in hand, Henry made many appointments and we visited various buyers and television stations. There was lots of interest but no bites. Two years after we had come up with the idea, it looked like it was about to become a reality. Erik Dwyer, commissioning editor of SBS, had built up SBS as Australia's premier food channel, with a diverse and brilliant range of chefs on show, and he gave us the go ahead! We were honoured to be accepted. We were going to make a TV show!

We were green, but in good hands. I was familiar with Sri Lanka but had no experience of working with a film crew and of the many obstacles to filming in a foreign land. I was setting off on another adventure in my culinary life. Learning a new angle on my passion for food and cooking and being able to focus on my ancestral home was a very exciting next step in my career.

ISLAND *Hopping*

In this book I will take you on a journey of flavours and skim along the ancient spice routes through the Pacific and to Sri Lanka. It is food that is easy to prepare, cost effective and tasty. The following recipes come from my television shows *My Sri Lanka* and *Island Feast*.

Experience and imagination is what I used to come up with these recipes, along with a lot of local knowledge. Talking to people is the best way to discover their passion, and when it comes to food, passion is everything. For filming, I made a point of arriving at each destination with only my knives and a chopping board. All of the ingredients I used were from the region. It was a challenge sometimes but it made me aware of what a large percentage of the world's population goes through every day. It also made the people from those areas very proud that I was using their produce. The following are brief cuisine descriptions of the food included in this book. (For a more detailed description of specific ingredients, please refer to the glossary on page 246.)

Sri Lanka

Sri Lankan food, to me, is a healthy vegetarian and rice-based cuisine. It is varied, unique in its preparation and cares for the main ingredient in every dish while allowing the cook to add their own flair. The food differs from city to city and has many ethnic influences. The Dutch, English, Tamils, Muslims and many others have had a hand in the evolution of this great cuisine. Many recipes are never written down but are instead passed on through families by word of mouth.

The foundation to any Sri Lankan meal begins with its curries. You can curry anything, and a Sri Lankan curry can be searing hot to delicately mild, but its flavours are like no other.

The Philippines

Filipino cuisine takes its influences from a number of cultures, mainly Chinese and Spanish. Before Spanish colonies settled in the region, the produce available in the Philippines, as well as the methods used to cook it, came from neighbouring China. Rice was widely cultivated and ingredients such as soy sauce, tofu and bean sprouts were traded into the Philippines. When the Spanish arrived, they brought supplies from the Americas, such as corn, tomatoes and potatoes, and introduced different styles of cooking, such as frying. The Filipino *longganisa* sausage (see page 109) is very similar to the Spanish chorizo. Today the Philippines is known for its sweet, sour and salty cuisine and communal way of eating.

Vanuatu

Vanuatu gained independence in 1980 so its cuisine is undoubtedly influenced by the British and French culture of its earlier controllers. Local specialties even include escargot; however, the group of islands that makes up Vanuatu mainly use local ingredients to create a distinctly tropical cuisine. Seafood is a common staple in the Pacific Islands and is widely available due to the abundance of beaches. Lobster, crabs, prawns and various types of fish are found as the main protein in many dishes. Fruits such as coconut, papaya, banana and mango are common, as are root vegetables, such as cassava and taro. Vanuatu also has a traditional drink called kava, made from the roots of the kava plant, which has mild narcotic effects.

Indonesia

Indonesian cuisine is immensely diverse as the nation comrises about 17,000 islands. Influences come from the Middle East, India, China and various parts of Europe, but these vary according to the Indonesian region. Although the nation's cuisine differs from island to island, rice is a staple ingredient throughout and is served with most meals as a side dish. Sambals (see pages 174–182) made with different spices and other flavourings are also a popular accompaniment to many Indonesian dishes. A number of other ingredients are used in many parts of Indonesia, such as peanuts (in peanut sauce), coconut, different types of chillies and palm sugar.

Cook Islands

The food of the Cook Islands largely centres on the fresh tropical ingredients that are abundantly available. Seafood is cooked in myriad ways, commonly underground in an earth oven known as an *umu* (see page 148). Raw fish is also popular, such as in the classic *ika mata* (see page 32). Staple ingredients also include papaya, coconut, cassava, breadfruit and taro, which is grown in many parts of the Cook Islands. An alcoholic home brew made of oranges, malt, yeast and sugar is popular among men, who gather at their local *tumunu* (bush pub) to drink it.

Snacks and Street Food

CORNET OF BLACK PEPPER BEEF

PASSING AROUND A LARGE PLATTER OF THESE BETEL LEAVES IS A GREAT WAY TO START A PARTY. WHEN WE WERE IN MATALE FILMING *MY SRI LANKA*, THESE SNACKS WERE CREATED UNDER GREAT DURESS. ALTHOUGH THE FOOTAGE OF COOKING THIS DISH WAS STUNNING, IT HAD BEEN RAINING FOR THE PAST WEEK, THE COUNTRY WAS IN TURMOIL, PEOPLE WERE DISPLACED AND THERE WERE LANDSLIDES AND FLOODS EVERYWHERE. WE WERE AT A PEPPER AND VANILLA PLANTATION AND WHAT YOU COULD NOT SEE WAS THAT OUR SHOES WERE COMPLETELY SUBMERGED IN THE MUD — THE MAGIC OF TELEVISION MADE THE BACKDROP LOOK IDYLLIC.

MAKES 12

250 g (9 oz) beef fillet or trimmed sirloin, thinly sliced against the grain
3 kochi chillies or hot green chillies, thinly sliced
juice of 1 lime
50 g (1¾ oz) cracked black peppercorns
½ teaspoon salt
12 betel leaves (see glossary)
1 teaspoon fresh or tinned green peppercorns
100 ml (3½ fl oz) vegetable oil
3 garlic cloves
1 sprig curry leaves, leaves picked
½ onion, thinly sliced

TO GARNISH
2 tomatoes, seeds removed and thinly sliced
1 red capsicum (pepper), seeds removed and thinly sliced
1 small cucumber, peeled, seeds removed and sliced into thin batons
2 French shallots, sliced
¼ bunch coriander (cilantro), leaves picked
2 spring onions (scallions), cut into 10 cm (4 inch) lengths

Place the beef, chilli and lime juice in a bowl and toss to coat. Add the black peppercorns and salt and toss again. Set aside to marinate for 5 minutes.

Meanwhile, prepare the betel leaves. Form a leaf, presentation side facing out, into a cone shape and secure with a toothpick. Repeat with the remaining leaves.

Add the green peppercorns to the beef and stir to combine.

Heat the oil in a wok over high heat. When the oil is very hot, add the garlic, curry leaves and onion. Once the garlic has browned, add the beef and stir constantly, making sure the heat of the wok doesn't decrease. Remove the beef from the wok after a few minutes or once it has browned.

To serve, place a small portion of the beef in each betel leaf cone and insert the tomato, capsicum, cucumber, shallot, coriander and spring onion inside.

PRAWN AND SWEET POTATO ROLLS

MAKES 10

2 eggs, lightly beaten
150 g (5 oz/1 cup) plain (all-purpose) flour, for dusting
300 g (10 ½ oz/3 cups) dried fine breadcrumbs
vegetable oil, for deep-frying
tomato sambal (see page 177), to serve
lime halves, to serve

SAVOURY FILLING

1 kg (2 lb 3 oz) sweet potato (yam), roughly chopped
200 ml (7 fl oz) vegetable oil
2 cm (¾ inch) piece of ginger, finely chopped
3 garlic cloves, finely chopped
1 red onion, finely diced
2 small green chillies, finely chopped
2 sprigs curry leaves, leaves picked
1 heaped teaspoon ground coriander
1 teaspoon red chilli powder
1 teaspoon fennel seeds
½ teaspoon ground cumin
¼ teaspoon fenugreek seeds, lightly toasted
½ teaspoon salt
300 g (10 ½ oz) prawn (shrimp) meat, roughly chopped

PANCAKE BATTER

4 eggs
450 ml (16 fl oz) milk
500 g (1 lb 2 oz/3 ⅓) cups plain (all-purpose) flour, sifted
2 tablespoons vegetable oil, plus extra for cooking

To make the savoury filling, place the sweet potato in a saucepan, cover with plenty of cold water, bring to the boil over medium heat and cook for 15 minutes or until tender. Drain, then return to the pan.

Heat the oil in a saucepan over high heat, add the ginger, garlic, onion, green chilli and curry leaves and cook until the onion is softened and translucent.

Add the spices and salt and cook, stirring so the spices don't burn, until fragrant. Add the prawn meat and cook until sealed all over.

Add the prawn mixture to the sweet potato and mash until well combined. Set aside.

Meanwhile, to make the pancake batter, whisk the eggs and milk in a large bowl until well combined. While whisking, gradually add the flour and whisk well to ensure there are no lumps. Stir in the oil, then set the batter aside to rest.

To cook the pancakes, heat a little oil in a non-stick frying pan over high heat. The pan needs to be hot, but not so hot that the pancakes burn — you don't want too much colour on the pancakes. Once the oil is hot, spoon a ladleful, about ¼ cup, of the batter into the pan and swirl to coat the base. Once the pancake is loose enough to come away from the pan, flip it over and cook the other side. Remove from the pan and repeat with the remaining batter.

To assemble the rolls, lay a pancake on a work surface, place a small amount of the savoury filling in the centre, fold two opposite sides of the pancake over the filling and roll up like a spring roll to enclose the filling completely. Use some of the beaten egg to help the edges stick if necessary. Repeat with the remaining pancakes and filling.

Place the flour, beaten egg and breadcrumbs in separate shallow bowls and line up in a row. Coat each in flour, dip in the beaten egg, shaking off any excess, then coat in the breadcrumbs and place on a tray.

To cook the rolls, fill a deep-sided saucepan one-third full of oil and heat to 180ºC (360ºF) or until a cube of bread turns golden in 15 seconds. Deep-fry the rolls, in batches, until crisp and golden all over. Remove with a slotted spoon and drain on paper towel.

Serve hot or at room temperature with the tomato sambal and lime halves.

BARBECUED PORK BELLY SKEWERS

EVERYWHERE YOU TRAVEL IN THE PHILIPPINES YOU WILL SEE SMALL BARBECUE SET-UPS OUTSIDE SHOPS SELLING THIS TRADITIONAL SNACK. IT IS ALWAYS NICE TO SIT DOWN FOR A FEW MINUTES, HAVE A CONVERSATION WITH THE STORE OWNER AND TAKE IN WHAT IS HAPPENING AROUND YOU. THE SECRET TO WHAT MAKES THESE BARBECUED SKEWERS UNIQUE AND SO TASTY IS THE USE OF LEMONADE. THIS TENDERISES THE MEAT AND ADDS FLAVOUR TO THE MARINADE. IT DOES MAKE A STICKY MESS OF YOUR GRILL BUT THE TASTE IS WELL WORTH IT. IF YOU FIND THE SWEETNESS OF THE LEMONADE TOO INTENSE, SERVE WITH THE CANE VINEGAR DIP (SEE PAGE 193) TO BALANCE IT OUT.

SERVES 4–6

1 kg (2 lb 3 oz) boneless pork belly, skin removed
1 small head garlic, peeled and minced
1 onion, finely chopped
55 g (2 oz/¼ cup firmly packed) soft brown sugar or white sugar
1 teaspoon ground black pepper
250 ml (8 ½ fl oz/1 cup) soy sauce
125 ml (4 fl oz/½ cup) tomato sauce (ketchup)
125 ml (4 fl oz/½ cup) lemonade or beer (optional)
60 ml (2 fl oz/¼ cup) calamansi juice (see glossary) or lemon juice
20 bamboo skewers, soaked in water for 30 minutes

Cut the pork into long, thin slices, about 5 mm (¼ inch) thick and 5 cm (2 inches) wide and place in a large bowl. Add the garlic, onion, sugar, pepper, soy sauce, tomato sauce, lemonade and calamansi juice and combine well using your hands. Cover and refrigerate for at least 30 minutes, turning occasionally.

Preheat a charcoal barbecue or regular barbecue grill to medium.

Thread the pork strips onto the bamboo skewers, reserving the marinade.

Barbecue the skewers for about 10 minutes or until cooked through, turning and basting with the reserved marinade every few minutes.

From left to right: pani puri (see page 22) and prawn and lentil snacks (see page 23).

PANI PURI

THIS HEALTHY AND TASTY STREET FOOD SNACK IS FROM SRI LANKA. VENDORS CARRY EVERYTHING WITH THEM, INCLUDING A POT OF HOT OIL, AND THEY ARE FREE TO SET UP THEIR PANI PURI STATION ON ANY STREET CORNER. THIS IS A VEGETARIAN SNACK ORIGINALLY FROM NORTHERN INDIA WHERE PURI ARE CALLED GOLGAPPA.

MAKES 12 (PICTURED PAGE 20)

PANI

100 g (3½ oz) tamarind pulp (see glossary)
500 ml (17 fl oz/2 cups) water
100 g (3½ oz) mint leaves
1 teaspoon ground cumin, toasted
1 teaspoon crushed Indian black salt (see glossary)
½ teaspoon ground black pepper
a pinch of asafoetida (see glossary)
salt, to taste

PURI

250 g (9 oz/2 cups) fine semolina
a pinch of baking powder
½ teaspoon salt
100 ml (3½ fl oz) water, or just enough to
   make a stiff dough
100 ml (3½ fl oz) vegetable oil, plus extra for deep-frying

FILLING

4 potatoes, roughly chopped
1 teaspoon ground turmeric
1 small onion, finely chopped
2 tablespoons chopped coriander (cilantro)
1 tablespoon vegetable oil
1 teaspoon chilli flakes
½ teaspoon black mustard seeds
½ teaspoon salt
juice of ½ lime

To make the pani, soak the tamarind in half of the water for 2 hours, Mash with your fingertips, then strain the mixture into a bowl and reserve the tamarind water. Discard the solids.

Process the mint in a small food processor until finely chopped. Place the mint, tamarind water, cumin, black salt, pepper, asafoetida, salt and the remaining water in a large bowl and stir to combine. Set aside.

To make the puri, combine the semolina, baking powder, salt, water and oil in a bowl and knead for 5 minutes or until a hard dough forms. Cover with a damp cloth and leave for 2 hours.

Take golf ball-sized balls of the dough and roll into 5 mm (¼ inch) thick rounds like chapatis.

Heat 1 litre (34 fl oz/4 cups) of oil in a deep-sided saucepan to 180°C (360°F) or until a cube of bread turns golden in 15 seconds. Add the puri, in batches, and deep-fry on each side until golden, puffed up and crisp. Remove with a slotted spoon and drain on paper towel, making sure they are not piled on one another so that they stay crispy.

To make the filling, place the potato and turmeric in a saucepan of cold salted water, bring to the boil, then reduce to a simmer and cook until tender. Drain well and place in a large bowl.

Heat the oil in a small frying pan over medium heat, add the onion and cook until soft and translucent.

Add the onion to the potato along with the remaining ingredients and mash well to combine.

To serve, make a hole in the centre of a puri, fill with the filling, then dip the entire puri in the pani so that some of the liquid fills the puri. Eat in one bite.

PRAWN AND LENTIL SNACKS
ISSO VADAI

IF YOU TAKE A STROLL ALONG GALLE FACE GREEN, THE SEASIDE PROMENADE IN COLOMBO, SRI LANKA, YOU WILL FIND MANY VENDORS SELLING THIS TASTY SNACK. OUR DAD ALWAYS TOOK US THERE TO FLY OUR KITES AND RUN AROUND ON A SUNDAY AFTERNOON AND IT ALWAYS HAD THE FEELING OF A FUNFAIR TO ME. EATING THIS CRISPY SNACK ALWAYS BRINGS BACK THOSE SUNDAY MEMORIES.

DURING HIS CHILDHOOD MY DAD GOT VERY SICK AND HAD A LOT OF TROUBLE RECOVERING. ONE DAY, HIS DAD TOOK HIM TO GALLE FACE GREEN TO GET SOME SEA AIR AND HE SAW A GROUP OF YOUNG MEN WRESTLING ON THE BEACH. HE WAS INTERESTED IN WHAT THEY WERE DOING AND WHEN ONE OF THE BOYS ASKED HIM TO JOIN HE THOUGHT HE WOULD GIVE IT A TRY. HE BECAME A GREAT WRESTLER AND HIS SICKNESS ALSO WENT AWAY.

MAKES 24 (PICTURED PAGE 21)

200 g (7 oz/1 cup) split red lentils (dal)
2.5 cm (1 inch) piece of ginger
2 onions, chopped
4 small green chillies, chopped
1 tablespoon cumin seeds
6 curry leaves, finely shredded
12 coriander (cilantro) leaves, chopped
salt, to taste
500 g (1 lb 2 oz) raw school (very small)
   prawns (shrimp), unshelled
vegetable oil, for deep-frying

Soak half of the lentils in plenty of cold water for 2–3 hours.

Drain the lentils, place in a small food processor or blender with the ginger and coarsely grind.

Transfer to a bowl, add the remaining lentils, the onion, chilli, cumin, curry leaves and coriander, season with salt and mix well.

Using damp hands, roll the mixture into golf ball-sized balls, then flatten into patties. Push four or five whole prawns into each patty.

Fill a deep-sided saucepan or wok one-third full of oil and heat to 180°C (360°F) or until a cube of bread turns golden in 15 seconds. Deep-fry the patties, in batches, for 3–5 minutes or until crisp and golden. Remove with a slotted spoon and drain on paper towel. Serve hot or at room temperature.

STUFFED CAPSICUM CHILLIES

THIS IS A GREAT SNACK OR ACCOMPANIMENT TO A MEAL. THE FLAVOURS OF THE CAPSICUM AND THE STUFFING PAIR SO WELL. MY MUM IS AUSTRIAN AND THE FLAVOUR OF THESE CAPSICUMS BRING BACK SO MANY MEMORIES. IT WAS ONE OF MY FAVOURITE CHILDHOOD MEALS AND STILL IS TODAY. ALTHOUGH THE FLAVOURS IN THIS VERSION ARE SRI LANKAN, MY MUM USED TO STUFF THE CAPSICUMS WITH RICE AND MINCED MEAT AND COOK THEM IN A PRESSURE COOKER — AUSTRIAN STYLE.

SERVES 6

6 capsicum (peppers) chillies, halved lengthways and seeds removed
2 tablespoons vegetable oil
2 garlic cloves, chopped
2 small red onions, chopped
salt, to taste
1 tablespoon Maldive fish flakes (see glossary)
4-5 curry leaves
1 teaspoon Sri Lankan curry powder
½ teaspoon red chilli powder
1 thin slice of ginger
½ teaspoon ground turmeric
125 ml (4 fl oz/ ½ cup) coconut milk

Heat 1 tablespoon of the oil in a large saucepan over medium heat, add the garlic and cook for about 20 seconds. Add the onion, ginger, fish flakes, curry leaves, half of the curry powder and half of the chilli powder, season with salt and cook until the onion is golden.

Stuff the capsicum chilli halves with the onion mixture and set aside.

Mix the remaining curry powder and chilli powder, the turmeric and coconut milk in a bowl and season with a little bit of salt.

Heat the remaining oil in a large frying pan over medium-high heat, add the stuffed yellow chilli halves and cook for 2 minutes.

Add the coconut milk mixture to the pan and cook for 2 minutes or until heated through.

CHILLED KING PRAWNS WITH AIOLI AND LEMON

THIS IS A SIMPLE DISH THAT RELIES ON THE BEST QUALITY LARGE, FIRM PRAWNS YOU CAN FIND. DO NOT CHOOSE PRAWNS WITH BLACK OR DROOPY HEADS AND IF POSSIBLE, BUY THEM FROZEN AND DEFROST THEM UNDER COOL RUNNING WATER AS YOU NEED THEM. PRAWNS ARE AN EXPENSIVE PRODUCT, SO IT'S IMPORTANT TO HANDLE THEM WELL SO YOU GET THE BEST VALUE FOR MONEY. IF YOU'RE GOING OUT TO BUY PRAWNS OR ANY SEAFOOD, ENSURE YOU TAKE AN ICE BOX. AS SOON AS YOU HAVE PURCHASED YOUR SEAFOOD, PLACE IT IN ICE SO IT STAYS FRESH.

SERVES 6

6 large raw king prawns (shrimp)
    (about 500 g / 1 lb 2 oz), unshelled
lemon halves wrapped in muslin (cheesecloth), to serve
½ cup aioli (see page 189), to serve

Cook the prawns in boiling salted water for 3 minutes, then drain and refresh in iced water. Drain again. Peel and devein the prawns leaving the tails intact. Serve with the aioli for dipping and lemon halves for squeezing over.

EMPANADA SPECIAL

BORN FROM THE AMAZING MIX OF CULTURES THAT MAKES UP PINOY CUISINE, THIS EMPANADA IS ONE OF THE BEST FOODS I'VE EVER EATEN, AND THE RUNNY EGG YOLK INSIDE IS SUCH A TASTY SURPRISE. I EXPERIENCED THESE ONES IN VIGAN, A WORLD-HERITAGE LISTED CITY IN NORTHERN LUZON, IN THE PHILIPPINES. THE STREETS ARE COBBLESTONED AND THE ROADS ARE LINED WITH STORES SELLING COLLECTABLES FROM VIGAN'S SPANISH COLONIAL TIMES. AND YOU CAN TAKE THIS ALL IN WHILE RIDING IN YOUR OWN HORSE-DRAWN CART.

MAKES 12

12 lightly oiled banana leaves, trimmed to
   14 cm (5½ inch) squares, for rolling
vegetable oil, for deep-frying
cane vinegar dip (see page 193)

DOUGH
90 ml (3 fl oz) vegetable oil
1 teaspoon annatto seeds (see glossary)
150 g (5 oz) rice flour
150 g (5 oz/1 cup) plain (all-purpose) flour
120 ml (4 fl oz) water

FILLING
150 g (5 oz) cabbage, shredded
100 g (3½ oz) carrot, shredded
1 large brown onion, shredded
12 eggs
150 g (5 oz) longganisa sausage (see glossary) or
   chorizo sausage, casings removed and meat minced

To make the dough, place the oil and annatto seeds in a small saucepan over low heat and heat until just warm. Cool for 20 minutes, then strain through a fine mesh sieve into a bowl and discard the seeds. Cool to room temperature.

Place the flour in a bowl and make a well. Add the water and infused oil to the well and stir until a dough forms, then turn out and knead on a work surface (there's no need to dust as the oil will keep the dough from sticking) for 3–5 minutes or until pliable. Return to a clean bowl, cover and leave for 1 hour.

To make the filling, combine the cabbage, carrot and onion in a bowl. Separate the eggs, being careful not to break the yolks, and set each yolk aside in a separate cup (this will make it easier to handle when assembling). Add the eggwhite to the vegetable mixture and combine well.

To make the empanadas, divide the dough, vegetable mixture and minced sausage into 12 portions. Making one empanada at a time, roll out a portion of dough onto an oiled banana leaf into a nice thin round, about 12 cm (5 inches) in diameter. Arrange the vegetable mixture in a circle on the edge of the pastry, leaving a border on the outer edge, then place the minced sausage in the centre. Carefully place an egg yolk in the centre of the meat, then fold the empanada in half to make a semi-circle, pressing the edge to seal well. Set aside on its banana leaf base. Repeat with the remaining dough and fillings.

Fill a large deep-sided saucepan or wok two-thirds full of oil and heat to 180°C (360°F) or until a cube of bread turns golden in 15 seconds. To fry, dip the empanadas, one at a time, into the hot oil by holding the banana leaf in the oil until it separates from the empanada. Do not cook the leaf. Deep-fry until golden and crisp. Remove with a slotted spoon and drain on paper towel. Serve hot with the cane vinegar dip.

EGG ROLLS

THESE EGG ROLLS CAN BE FOUND ALL OVER SRI LANKA, BUT THIS VERSION, WITH A PERFECTLY COOKED EGG CRUSTED IN A SPICY FISH CURRY, COMES FROM GALLE IN THE SOUTH.

MAKES 8

4 eggs, hard-boiled, peeled and halved lengthways
300 ml (10 fl oz) vegetable oil

TUNA FILLING
200 g (7 oz) piece of tuna fillet (or drained tinned tuna)
½ teaspoon salt
1 tablespoon ground black pepper
400 g (14 oz) potatoes, roughly chopped

TEMPERED SPICES
100 ml (3½ fl oz) vegetable oil
1 teaspoon ground black pepper
2 small green chillies, finely chopped
1 small onion, finely chopped
1 sprig curry leaves, leaves picked
2 teaspoons curry powder
½ teaspoon red chilli powder
salt, to taste

PANCAKES
150 g (5 oz/1 cup) plain (all-purpose) flour
2 eggs
300 ml (10 fl oz) milk
vegetable oil, for cooking

CRUMBING MIXTURE
150 g (5 oz/1 cup) plain (all-purpose) flour
4 eggs
100 ml (3½ fl oz) water
300 g (10½ oz/3 cups) dried fine breadcrumbs

To make the tuna filling, place the tuna fillet (if using tinned tuna, skip this step), salt and pepper in a saucepan, add enough water to cover, place over medium heat and cook for 10 minutes or until cooked through. Drain and set aside.

Place the potato in a saucepan of cold water, bring to the boil and cook until tender. Drain and combine with the cooked (or tinned) tuna in a large bowl and mash until smooth. Check the seasoning and set aside.

To make the tempered spices, heat the oil in a frying pan over high heat. Once hot, add the pepper, chilli, onion and curry leaves and cook until the onion starts to brown. Add the curry powder and chilli powder. Remove from the heat and combine with the tuna mixture. Set aside.

To make the pancakes, whisk the flour, eggs, milk and 2 tablespoons of oil together in a large bowl until smooth and lump free. If the mixture is too thick, add a bit of water. Set aside for at least 10 minutes or until ready to cook.

Heat a little bit of oil in a non-stick frying pan over high heat. Once the oil is hot, spoon a ladleful of the batter into the pan and swirl to form a thin 20 cm (8 inch) diameter round. Once the pancake is loose enough to come away from the pan, flip it over and cook the other side. You don't want the pancake to be crisp — it should be still soft enough to fold without tearing. Remove from the pan and set aside. Repeat with the remaining batter. You will need 8 pancakes.

To make the crumbing mixture, whisk the flour, eggs and water together in a large bowl and set aside.

To assemble the rolls, lay a pancake on a work surface and place a small amount of the tuna filling in the centre. Place an egg half on top. Fold each side of the pancake into the centre to form a square parcel. Use some of the crumbing mixture to help the edges stick if necessary. Repeat with the remaining pancakes and filling. Coat each egg roll in the crumbing mixture, shaking off the excess, then roll in the breadcrumbs.

Fill a deep-sided saucepan or wok one-third full of oil and heat to 180°C (360°F) or until a cube of bread turns golden in 15 seconds. Deep-fry the rolls, in batches, until crisp and golden. Remove with a slotted spoon and drain on paper towel. Serve hot or at room temperature.

RAW FISH SALAD KOKODA

KOKODA IS A SEAFOOD SALAD, SIMILAR TO CEVICHE, MADE WITH FISH, TOMATO, COCONUT CREAM AND VARIOUS SPICES AND SEASONINGS. IT IS LOVED ALL OVER THE PACIFIC AND IS KNOWN AS *IKA MATA* IN THE COOK ISLANDS.

SERVES 6

1 rainbow runner fillet (about 1 kg/2 lb 3 oz),
    skinned and pin-boned (or you could use snapper,
    blue-eye trevalla or tuna)
juice of 2 large limes
1 small red onion, finely diced
4 small green chillies, chopped
20 g (¾ oz) candied nutmeg (see glossary), finely diced
3 vine-ripened tomatoes, peeled and diced
250 ml (8½ fl oz/1 cup) coconut cream
1 teaspoon cracked black pepper
salt, to taste
½ bunch coriander (cilantro), sprigs picked, to serve

Cut the fish into 1 cm (⅜ inch) pieces and place in a bowl with the lime juice. Toss to coat and leave for 30 minutes or until the fish turns opaque.

   Add the onion, chilli, candied nutmeg and tomato and combine well.

   Add the coconut cream and pepper and season with salt. Serve immediately, scattered with the coriander.

BUTTER-FRIED CAULIFLOWER

CAULIFLOWER REALLY ISN'T EATEN AS MUCH AS IT SHOULD BE. IN SRI LANKAN COOKERY THE CAULIFLOWER IS LOVED. IT HAS A GREAT TEXTURE AND FLAVOUR AND TAKES TO SPICE WELL. I USED TO LOVE FINDING BEAUTIFUL LITTLE PERFECT CAULIFLOWERS WHEN SHOPPING WITH MY AUNTIES.

SERVES 6

500 g (1 lb 2 oz) cauliflower, cut into florets
40–60 g (1½–2 oz) butter
1 teaspoon brown mustard seeds
2 garlic cloves, finely chopped
1 small onion, finely chopped
½ teaspoon ground turmeric
2 tablespoons chopped coriander (cilantro)
½ teaspoon chilli flakes, or if you want it hot, you can add more
2 small green chillies, chopped
salt and ground black pepper, to taste
150 g (5 oz/1 cup) frozen peas

Bring a saucepan of water to the boil. Add the cauliflower and cook for 5 minutes or until tender. Drain and set aside.

Melt the butter in a frying pan over medium heat, add the mustard seeds, garlic and onion and cook until soft and translucent.

Add the turmeric and then the cauliflower and stir to mix well. Add the chilli flakes and green chilli, season with salt and pepper and stir well. Simmer for 5–8 minutes, adding the peas in the last few minutes of cooking.

BITTER GOURD WITH EGGS

THE BITTER GOURD, PRIZED FOR ITS HEALTH QUALITIES, IS MADE INTO AN OMELETTE HERE. AFTER SALTING, A LOT OF THE BITTERNESS IS REMOVED BUT MAKE SURE NOT TO OVERCOOK IT SO THAT ITS MEDICINAL VALUE REMAINS INTACT.

SERVES 4

225 g (8 oz) bitter gourd (see glossary)
500 ml (17 fl oz/2 cups) water
1 tablespoon salt
1 spring onion (scallion)
80 ml (2 fl oz/⅓ cup) vegetable oil
6 garlic cloves, minced
2 onions, thinly sliced
3 small tomatoes, chopped
2 small green chillies, chopped
3 large eggs, lightly beaten

Trim away the pointed ends of the gourd and halve lengthways. Remove the pale seeds with a spoon and discard. Cut each half into 5 mm (¼ inch) thick slices on the diagonal.

Place the water in a large bowl, dissolve the salt and add the gourd. Set aside for 2 hours. Drain the gourd and rinse under running water. Drain again and pat dry.

Cut the spring onion into 5 cm (2 inch) lengths, then cut each section lengthways into thin strips. Set aside.

Heat the oil in a large frying pan over medium heat. When hot, add the garlic and cook until lightly golden. Add the onion and cook for 2 minutes. Add the tomato and chilli and cook for 2 minutes.

Add the gourd, reduce the heat to medium and cook, stirring occasionally, for 3 minutes or until the gourd is tender.

Stir in the beaten eggs, season with salt and cook as you would scrambled eggs until it is the consistency you like. Remove from the heat, add the spring onion and serve.

JASMINE-SCENTED STEAMED PRAWNS

COOKING WITH TEA IS A GREAT WAY TO SCENT FOOD. TEA SMOKING HAS LONG BEEN THE NORM, BUT HERE I'VE SCENTED THE STEAMING LIQUID WITH TEA AND IT WORKS A TREAT. THE GENTLE STEAMING ADDS A DELICATE FRAGRANCE WITHOUT OVERWHELMING THE SWEET TASTE OF THE PRAWNS.

SERVES 4

125 ml (4 fl oz/½ cup) olive oil
2 teaspoons rice vinegar
1 jalapeño chilli, finely chopped
1 tablespoon minced garlic
pinch of ground black pepper
1 tablespoon finely shredded coriander (cilantro)
1 tablespoon green tea leaves with jasmine flowers
2 litres (4 pt 4 fl oz) water
16 large raw prawns (shrimp), shelled and deveined
   with the tails intact
thinly sliced red radish, to garnish

Whisk the oil, vinegar, chilli, garlic, pepper and coriander in a bowl to combine.

Heat the water in a double boiler, bring to the boil and add the tea. Place the prawns in the steamer basket, cover and steam for 3 minutes or until the prawns are cooked.

Place the prawns and radish in a bowl, drizzle with the dressing and toss to combine. Serve immediately.

DUTCH FORCED MEATBALLS
FRIKKADELS

THESE ARE SRI LANKAN DUTCH-INFLUENCED MEATBALLS AND A FAVOURITE OF THE BURGHER COMMUNITY. I LOVE THIS SNACK AND THERE ARE MANY VERSIONS ALL OVER THE WORLD WHEREVER THERE IS ANYONE WITH A BIT OF DUTCH BLOOD, SUCH AS SRI LANKA AND SOUTH AFRICA, AND EACH REGION HAS ITS OWN UNIQUE INTERPRETATION.

MAKES 24 / SERVES 6

450 g (1 lb) ground beef
1 teaspoon salt
1 teaspoon ground black pepper
½ teaspoon ground cinnamon
¼ teaspoon ground cloves
1 tablespoon chopped red onion
1 thick slice of bread, lightly toasted and grated
1 teaspoon fennel seeds, lightly toasted and finely ground
1 small pinch of crushed saffron threads
1 tablespoon chopped fennel
2 cm (¾ inch) piece of young ginger, chopped
3 garlic cloves, chopped
juice of ½ lime
4 eggs, lightly beaten
ghee (see glossary), for shallow-frying
200 g (7 oz/2 cups) dried fine breadcrumbs

Preheat the oven to 180°C (360°F/Gas 4) and line a baking tray with paper towel.

Place the beef in a large bowl, season with the salt, pepper, cloves and cinnamon. Add the onion and grated bread, fennel seeds, saffron, chopped fennel, ginger and garlic. Moisten with the lime juice and a half of the beaten egg and mix well using your hands to combine. Using damp hands, form the mixture into golf ball-sized balls.

Heat the ghee in a frying pan over medium heat. Dip the balls in the remaining beaten egg, shaking off the excess, roll in the breadcrumbs and shallow-fry, in batches, until golden all over. Remove with a slotted spoon, place on the prepared tray and bake for 5 minutes or until cooked through.

FRESHWATER PRAWNS WITH GARLIC

WHILE IN THE COOK ISLANDS, I MET AN OLD FRIEND, TIRI, WHO TOOK ME PRAWN FISHING WHERE THE FRESHWATER STREAMS COME OFF THE MOUNTAINS. WE WADED THROUGH THE COOL CLEAR STREAMS, BATTLING SWARMS OF MOSQUITOES, HUNTING FOR FRESHWATER PRAWNS. THEY ARE A LOCAL DELICACY AND NOT SOLD COMMERCIALLY. USING A HOMEMADE NET, WE WADED IN BETWEEN THE FALLEN TREES AND LEAF LITTER SCOOPING UP THESE MAGNIFICENT PRAWNS, WHICH ARE UNIQUE AS THEY HAVE VERY LONG ARMS WITH SHARP PINCERS ON THE END OF THEM. WHEN WE GOT BACK, I PLACED THEM IN SEAWATER TO KILL THEM PRIOR TO COOKING — AND THIS ALSO SEASONED THE PRAWNS. YOU CAN SUBSTITUTE ANY GOOD-QUALITY FRESH PRAWNS. LEAVE THE SHELLS ON FOR EXTRA FLAVOUR AND LET EVERYONE GET THEIR HANDS MESSY AT THE TABLE.

SERVES 4

50 ml (1¾ fl oz) olive oil
4 garlic cloves, crushed
1 kg (2 lb 3 oz) freshwater prawns (shrimp)
    or ocean prawns, unshelled
juice of 2 limes
100 g (3½ oz) butter, diced
salt and ground black pepper, to taste

Heat the oil in a large heavy-based frying pan over high heat, add the garlic and cook for 3 minutes or until fragrant and just starting to turn golden.

Add the prawns and cook, stirring constantly, for 3 minutes. Add the lime juice and mix well. Add the butter, allow it to melt and toss occasionally until the prawns are coated in a thick sauce. Do not cook for too long or the butter will split. Season with salt and pepper and serve with a cold beer.

FILIPINO-STYLE CEVICHE SPANNER CRAB KINILAW

A *KINILAW* IS DIFFERENT FROM CEVICHE IN THAT RATHER THAN MARINATING SEAFOOD IN VINEGAR OR LIME JUICE, IT IS MORE ABOUT WASHING IT THROUGH THE VINEGAR. TREATING LOCAL CUISINE WITH RESPECT IS VERY IMPORTANT TO ME, BUT THIS RUSTIC DISH OF KINILAW, ALTHOUGH DELICIOUS, NEEDED SOME TWEAKING. I ASKED THE LOCALS IF IT WAS PERMISSIBLE TO USE COOKED SEAFOOD INSTEAD OF THE MORE TYPICAL RAW SEAFOOD AND THEY SAID YES. I WANTED TO USE LOBSTER BUT THERE WAS NONE AVAILABLE. HOWEVER, SOMEONE TOLD ME THERE WERE LOTS OF *CUCARACHAS* — THAT TO ME MEANT COCKROACHES. BUT IN THE PHILIPPINES CUCARACHAS ARE SPANNER CRABS, WHICH TASTED FANTASTIC. IN KEEPING WITH A TRADITIONAL KINILAW, INSTEAD OF WASHING THE SEAFOOD WITH VINEGAR, I SIMPLY WASH THE CUCUMBER THROUGH IT.

SERVES 4

SPANNER CRAB SALAD
200 g (7 oz) spanner crab meat, picked through for shell
½ bunch baby spring onions (scallions), green part only, finely chopped
juice of 1 mandarin
50 ml (1¾ fl oz) extra virgin olive oil

TOMATO CONCASSE
6 ripe tomatoes, peeled, seeds removed and finely diced
½ bunch baby spring onions (scallions), sliced
50 ml (1¾ fl oz) extra virgin olive oil
juice of ½ lime

CHILLI VINAIGRETTE
1 green chilli, seeds removed and diced
2 French shallots, finely diced
1 teaspoon soft brown sugar
100 ml (3½ fl oz) cane vinegar (see glossary)
100 ml (3½ fl oz) extra virgin olive oil

TO SERVE
2 small mandarins, segmented
50 g (1¾ oz) fresh seaweed
2 wing beans (see glossary), sliced
4 zucchini (courgette) flowers, torn into petals
1 Lebanese (small) cucumber, thinly sliced
200 g (7 oz) freshly grated coconut (see glossary)

To make the spanner crab salad, combine all of the ingredients in a bowl and refrigerate until needed.

To make the tomato concasse, combine all of the ingredients in a bowl and set aside.

To make the chilli vinaigrette, place all of the ingredients in a bowl and stir until the sugar dissolves. Set aside.

To assemble, using two tablespoons, shape the crab salad into quenelles and place in an S-shape on a large plate. Scatter the tomato concasse, mandarin segments, seaweed, wing beans and torn zucchini petals about the plate. Toss the cucumber in the chilli vinaigrette, then place the slices on top of the concasse. Drizzle the plate with a little vinaigrette, scatter the coconut over and serve immediately.

DEVILLED CASHEW NUTS

THIS IS A SRI LANKAN FAVOURITE, BEST ENJOYED WITH A BEER ON A BALCONY WHILE WATCHING THE SUN GO DOWN. IT'S A CLASSIC HOTEL SNACK AND I LIKE TO JUDGE A HOTEL'S KITCHEN BY THEIR DEVILLED CASHEWS. THE CASHEW NUT IS ONE OF THE ONLY NUTS TO GROW OUTSIDE THE FRUIT. THE REASON CASHEW NUTS ARE SO EXPENSIVE IS BECAUSE THEY ARE VERY TRICKY TO HARVEST. THE NUT IS SURROUNDED IN A BLACK SKIN AND WHEN YOU CUT THE SKIN, A WHITE MILKY SUBSTANCE COMES OUT; IF YOU GET THIS LIQUID ON YOUR HANDS, IT BURNS, SO GREAT CAUTION IS NEEDED IN HARVESTING.

SERVES 4

100 ml (3 ½ fl oz) vegetable oil
300 g (10 ½ oz) raw unsalted cashew nuts
2 sprigs curry leaves, leaves picked
½ teaspoon red chilli powder
½ teaspoon salt
½ teaspoon ground black pepper

Heat the oil in a heavy-based saucepan over medium heat until a light smoke haze comes off it. Add the nuts and fry until golden.

Add the curry leaves and cook until crisp and then strain through a fine mesh sieve into a heatproof bowl. Discard the oil. Place the nuts and curry leaves in a bowl.

Combine the chilli powder, salt and pepper. Toss the nuts and curry leaves in the mixture to coat well.

Soups
and Curries

CEYLON TEA PRAWNS WITH MULLIGATAWNY SOUP

THIS HOT PEPPER SOUP IS EATEN ALL OVER SRI LANKA BUT IS A PARTICULAR FAVOURITE OF THE TAMIL COMMUNITY IN THE NORTH. SERVED WITH BUTTERFLIED PRAWNS, THIS DISH IS ELEGANT AND ALWAYS IMPRESSES, YET IT IS SO EASY TO PREPARE.

SERVES 4

12 raw prawns (shrimp), shelled and deveined, shells reserved to make the stock
12 bamboo skewers, soaked in water for 30 minutes
vegetable oil, for brushing

STOCK
1 sprig curry leaves
1 garlic clove
1 small green chilli
1 red bird's eye chilli
2 cm (¾ inch) piece of ginger, roughly chopped
2 onions, roughly chopped
2 litres (4 pt 4 fl oz) water

MULLIGATAWNY SOUP
60 ml (2 fl oz/¼ cup) vegetable oil
1 sprig curry leaves, leaves picked
2 garlic cloves, finely chopped
1 onion, finely diced
1 long red chilli
2 teaspoons ground black pepper
1 teaspoon ground coriander
1 teaspoon red chilli powder
½ teaspoon ground cumin, toasted
½ teaspoon fennel seeds, toasted and ground
½ teaspoon ground turmeric
¼ teaspoon fenugreek seeds, toasted
pinch of saffron threads
2 carrots, finely diced
1 eggplant (aubergine), finely diced
1 tomato, finely diced
1 onion, finely chopped
salt and ground black pepper, to taste
juice of 1 lime

DIPPING SAUCE
2 tablespoons mayonnaise
2 garlic cloves, chopped
1 dried red chilli, crushed
¼ cup flat-leaf (Italian) parsley leaves, finely chopped
1 teaspoon Ceylon tea leaves

continued next page

continued from previous page

To make the stock, place the reserved prawn shells, the curry leaves, garlic, chilli, ginger, onion and water in a large saucepan and bring to the boil, then reduce the heat to a simmer and cook for 15 minutes.

To make the mulligatawny soup, heat 2 tablespoons of the oil in a large saucepan over high heat, add half of the curry leaves, garlic, onion, chilli and spices and cook until fragrant, stirring frequently making sure the spices don't burn.

Add the curry leaf mixture to the stock, increase the heat and bring to the boil, then reduce the heat to a simmer and cook, stirring occasionally, for a maximum of 20 minutes.

In the same pan that you used to fry the spices, heat the remaining oil over medium heat, add the carrot, eggplant, tomato and onion and gently cook for 4–5 minutes. Add the remaining curry leaves and stir to combine.

Strain the stock into the vegetable mixture, bring to the boil, then season with salt and pepper and add the lime juice. Remove from the heat and keep warm until serving.

To make the dipping sauce, place the mayonnaise, garlic, dried chilli and parsley in a bowl and stir to combine.

Place the tea in a small frying pan over high heat and lightly toast, being careful not to burn it. Remove from the heat and add a small amount to the mayonnaise mixture. Reserve the rest for garnishing.

Place each prawn on its back and lightly score the belly two or three times so that it lies flat. Remove the small spike between the two tail fins. Thread each prawn onto a skewer, starting at the head and through the tail.

Preheat a barbecue hotplate to high and lightly brush with oil. Cook the prawns until just translucent.

Coat each prawn in the dipping sauce, scatter with the remaining toasted tea leaves and serve with a bowl of soup and some of the strained vegetables if desired.

TOMATO CONSOMMÉ WITH BASIL

THIS LIGHT BROTH IS FULL OF FLAVOUR WITH A TINGE OF ROSY REDNESS. FOR THE BEST RESULTS, ALWAYS USE RIPE BUT FIRM TOMATOES AT THE PEAK OF THEIR SEASON. THE TRICK TO A CLEAR CONSOMMÉ, IS TO LEAVE IT TO HANG OVERNIGHT AND LET THE LIQUID DRIP OFF SLOWLY. THIS BROTH IS A GREAT OPTION FOR VEGETARIANS AND I USE IT IN SRI LANKAN COOKING WHEN MAKING VEGETABLE-BASED CURRIES.

SERVES 6

2.5 kg (5½ lb) ripe tomatoes
125 ml (4 fl oz/½ cup) vodka
½ cup basil leaves
2 garlic cloves
2 tablespoons freshly grated horseradish
1 tablespoon red wine vinegar
salt, to taste

Blend all of the ingredients together in a food processor until smooth. Strain the mixture through a fine mesh sieve lined with muslin (cheesecloth) or filter paper placed over a deep bowl. Do not push down on the solids. Leave the mixture to hang overnight in the refrigerator.

Discard the solids and serve the consommé chilled as a light starter or use it as a base for other dishes.

JAFFNA KOOL

COOL BY NAME AND SPICY BY FLAVOUR, THIS UNUSUAL DISH IS THE PRIDE AND JOY OF THE FISHERMEN FROM JAFFNA IN THE NORTH-WEST OF SRI LANKA. ALL OF THE INGREDIENTS COME FROM THE JAFFNA REGION.

SERVES 6

SOUP

100 g (3½ oz) palmyra flour (see glossary)
1.1 litres (42 pt 6 fl oz) water
¼ cup sambar rice (see glossary)
1 young jackfruit (see glossary), roughly chopped with ¼ seeds reserved
2 blue swimmer crabs
10 tiger prawns (shrimp), shelled and deveined
6 whiting fillets, bones removed
3 cleaned squid hoods (about 80 g/3 oz each)
1 teaspoon salt
1 teaspoon ground black pepper
¼ bunch snake (yard-long) beans
300 g (10½ oz) clams (vongole), purged of grit and steamed opened
¼ cup drumstick leaves (see glossary)

CHILLI PASTE

6 dried red chillies
juice of 1 lime
½ teaspoon salt
1 teaspoon ground black pepper

TAMARIND WATER

1 golf ball-sized piece of tamarind pulp (see glossary)
125 ml (4 fl oz/½ cup) water

To make the soup, place the palmyra flour and 100 ml (3½ fl oz) of the water in a bowl and leave to soak for about 1 hour or until the mixture forms a paste. Set aside until ready to use.

To make the chilli paste, place the dried chillies in a small bowl with enough hot water to cover and soak for 5–6 minutes. Drain, place in a blender with the lime juice, salt and pepper and blend for 30 seconds or until a paste forms. Set aside until ready to use.

To make the tamarind water, combine the tamarind and water in a small bowl and mix until it forms a thick paste. Strain through a fine mesh sieve, extracting as much liquid as possible. Discard the solids. Set aside until ready to use.

Place the remaining water, the rice and jackfruit seeds in a large saucepan over medium heat, cover and cook for 7–8 minutes or until the jackfruit seeds start to float.

Meanwhile, prepare the seafood. Pull off the top shell of the crabs, pull out the spongy grey gills and remove the guts. Chop the crab into quarters and slightly crack the legs. Shell the prawns and devein. Cut the fish into four to five pieces. Cut the squid into even chunks.

Add the jackfruit flesh to the rice mixture, stir to combine, increase the heat and bring to the boil. Once it starts to boil, add the crab, stir to combine, cover and boil for a few minutes or until the crab starts to turn pink.

Add the fish, cover and cook until the fish starts to turn white. Add the squid and prawns, stir once very gently so as not to break up the seafood, season with salt and pepper, then add the snake beans and a small amount of the chilli paste, cover and boil for 3 minutes.

Remove all of the seafood from the pan and set aside in a large bowl. Add a small amount of the tamarind water to the soup and check the taste. Add more if you prefer it more sour.

Add ¼ cup of the flour paste to the soup and stir to combine. Continue to boil until the soup is thick and glossy.

Return the seafood to the pan, along with the clams and drumstick leaves, stir once to combine and then check the flavour balance, adding extra tamarind water, chilli paste or salt and pepper if needed. Remove from the heat and serve.

DAL SOUP

DAL IS A STAPLE IN MANY ASIAN COUNTRIES. THIS VERSION IS SOUPY AND THIN. IT WARMS YOU IN WINTER AND GIVES YOU ENERGY. THE TEMPERING OF THE GARLIC, GINGER AND MUSTARD SEEDS ADDS A WONDERFUL RICH NOTE, AND GHEE ADDS THAT FLAVOUR THAT YOU CAN TASTE IN INDIAN FOOD, BUT YOU'RE NOT SURE WHAT IT IS. THIS IS AN IDEAL VEGETARIAN STARTER OR PERFECT AS AN ACCOMPANIMENT TO CURRIES.

SERVES 6

1 cup red lentils
1 teaspoon ground turmeric
2 dried long red chillies
1 red onion, finely chopped
1 vine-ripened tomato, chopped
1.5 litres (3 pt 3 fl oz) water
2 garlic cloves
5 cm (2 inch) piece of ginger, chopped
1 teaspoon cumin seeds
50 g (1¾ oz) ghee (see glossary)
1 sprig curry leaves, leaves picked
2 teaspoons black mustard seeds
salt and ground black pepper, to taste

Place the lentils, turmeric, chilli, onion, tomato and water in a saucepan, bring to the boil, then reduce the heat to a simmer and cook for 15 minutes or until the lentils are tender and beginning to break up.

Meanwhile, using a mortar and pestle, grind the garlic, ginger and cumin seeds into a paste.

Heat the ghee in a small heavy-based frying pan over medium–low heat, add the curry leaves, mustard seeds and the spice paste and cook for 4 minutes or just until the mustard seeds begin to pop and the mixture starts to brown.

Pour the spice mixture into the lentils, combine well and simmer for 4 minutes. Season with salt and pepper, then ladle into bowls to serve.

FILIPINO SOUR SOUP SEAFOOD SINIGANG

THIS IS A TRADITIONAL FILIPINO STEW CONTAINING SEAFOOD AND VEGETABLES, WITH A STRONG TAMARIND FLAVOUR. WHEN I FIRST CAME ACROSS THIS DISH, I IMMEDIATELY FELL IN LOVE WITH IT. I PROBABLY DO NOT ADD ENOUGH TAMARIND TO SUIT PINOY TASTES, BUT INSTEAD I HAVE ADJUSTED IT TO SUIT WESTERN PALATES. FEEL FREE TO MAKE IT MORE SOUR IF YOU WISH. THE SECRET IS, AS WITH MOST SOUPS, THE STOCK — IT SHOULD BE A CLEAR AND FLAVOURSOME BROTH.

SERVES 6

1 large snapper (about 1.4 kg/3 lb), filleted and skinned, bones reserved

salt, to taste

12 large raw tiger prawns (shrimp), shelled and deveined with tails and heads left intact

2 squid, cleaned, each cut into 6 pieces and scored in a crisscross pattern

30 ml (1 fl oz) fish sauce

STOCK

1 sprig curry leaves

4 cm (1½ inch) piece of ginger

1 head garlic

1 red onion, quartered

4 pods fresh green tamarind or 1 golf ball-sized ball tamarind pulp (see glossary)

½ teaspoon black peppercorns

salt, to taste

ACCOMPANIMENTS

4 tomatoes, quartered and seeds removed

12 baby leeks, trimmed and left whole

1 bunch Chinese broccoli or similar Asian green vegetable, trimmed

6 small green chillies

12 red Asian shallots, halved

1 white radish (daikon), peeled and cut into thin batons

To make the stock, wash the reserved fish bones and place in a large saucepan with all of the stock ingredients, except the salt. Bring to the boil over high heat, then reduce the heat to low and cook, skimming frequently, for 20 minutes.

Remove from the heat and leave for 10 minutes to allow the sediment to settle. Double strain the stock through a fine mesh sieve, discarding the solids. If the stock is still not clear, pass it through muslin (cheesecloth). Return to a clean pan, season with salt and bring to a simmer.

Blanch each type of seafood and each accompaniment separately in the stock and set aside.

If serving immediately, place a teaspoon of fish sauce in each serving bowl, divide the blanched ingredients among the bowls, pour over the stock and serve immediately. Alternatively, you can blanch everything beforehand, then reheat in the stock just before serving.

JAFFNA CRAB CURRY

NOW THAT THE CIVIL WAR IS OVER IN SRI LANKA, THE PEOPLE ARE RETURNING TO CLAIM THEIR ANCESTRAL LAND. ON DELF ISLAND, DESPITE THE RAVAGES OF WAR, NOT MUCH HAS CHANGED AND THE PEOPLE CONTINUE TO CELEBRATE THEIR FOOD TRADITIONS. THERE I FOUND A WONDERFUL LADY WHO TAUGHT ME HOW TO MAKE THE BEST CRAB CURRY ON THE PLANET. THE TIME AND EFFORT SHE SPENT IN GRINDING THE COCONUT WAS PRAISEWORTHY. HER PASTE WAS INCREDIBLY TOASTY AND RICH. IF YOU DON'T HAVE TIME TO GRIND THE PASTE BY HAND, A BLENDER DOES THE JOB NICELY.

SERVES 4–6

2 live mud crabs (about 1.2 kg / 2 lb 10 oz each)
2 teaspoons cumin seeds
½ cup freshly grated coconut
1 teaspoon black peppercorns, ground
1 golf ball-sized piece tamarind pulp (see glossary)
400 ml (13½ fl oz) coconut milk
50 g (1¾ oz) ghee (see glossary)
1 teaspoon black mustard seeds
1 teaspoon fennel seeds
1 red onion, sliced
1 sprig curry leaves, leaves picked
3 small green chillies, finely chopped

1 tablespoon Jaffna curry powder (see glossary)
1 tablespoon red chilli powder
¼ teaspoon ground turmeric
500 ml (17 fl oz / 2 cups) water
1 sprig drumstick leaves (see glossary)
juice of ½ lime
salt, to taste
coriander (cilantro) leaves, to garnish

Put the crabs in the freezer for 1 hour to immobilise them or in a bucket of iced water for 15 minutes. Pull off the top shells, pull out the spongy grey gills and remove the guts. Chop the crab into 6 pieces and crack the large claws but leave them attached.

In a dry frying pan over medium heat, toast the cumin seeds, coconut and pepper until the coconut is golden. Grind to a smooth paste using a large mortar and pestle or in a blender and set aside.

Combine the tamarind and coconut milk in a small bowl and mix until it forms a thick paste. Strain through a fine mesh sieve, extracting as much liquid as possible. Discard the solids. Set aside until ready to use.

Heat the ghee in a large heavy-based saucepan over high heat, add the mustard seeds and cook until they start to pop, then add the fennel seeds and cook until they are lightly toasted. Add the onion, curry leaves and chilli and cook for a few minutes or until the onion is golden.

Add the curry powder, chilli powder and turmeric and mix in. Add the crab and cook for 3 minutes. At this stage you need to stir it a lot so the spices don't burn. Add the coconut paste, stir and add the water. If the curry is too dry, add more water. Cover and simmer for 12 minutes or until the crab is just cooked through and the sauce has thickened.

Add the tamarind liquid, stir through and bring back to the boil.

Remove from the heat, stir in the drumstick leaves and lime juice and season with salt. Garnish with the coriander to serve.

LAMB CURRY

MY DAD ALWAYS COOKED THIS FLAVOURSOME CURRY AND OUR FAMILY LOVED IT. WHEN WE FIRST ARRIVED IN AUSTRALIA, WE WERE BROKE AND EVERYTHING SEEMED TO BE EXPENSIVE, ESPECIALLY MEAT. DAD'S MOTTO WAS THE MORE BONES THE BETTER AND HE ALWAYS USED BARBECUE CHOPS WHEN MAKING THIS CURRY — THE BONES SEEM TO HOLD THE LUSCIOUS GRAVY TO THE MEAT, MAKING IT UNBELIEVABLY MOREISH.

SERVES 6

400 g (14 oz) lamb, preferably barbecue chops with bones, chopped into 2 cm (¾ inch) pieces
100 g (3½ oz) onion, diced
1 sprig curry leaves, leaves picked
2 garlic cloves
2 thin slices of ginger
10 cm (4 inch) piece of lemongrass
1 cinnamon stick
2 teaspoons ground coriander, roasted
2 teaspoons roasted ground fennel seeds
2 teaspoons ground cumin
1 teaspoon toasted and ground cumin seeds
½ teaspoon fenugreek seeds, lightly toasted
½ teaspoon ground turmeric
½ teaspoon red chilli powder
1 litre (34 fl oz/4 cups) water
200 ml (7 fl oz) coconut cream
juice of ½ lime
1 teaspoon salt

Place the lamb, onion, curry leaves, garlic, ginger, lemongrass, all of the spices and water in a heavy-based saucepan, bring to the boil, then reduce the heat to a simmer and cook for 30 minutes or until the sauce thickens and the meat is tender. Add the coconut cream and bring to the boil. Remove from the heat, stir through the lime juice and season with salt.

Fausi's tuna curry

I TRULY BELIEVE THE EPISODE OF *ISLAND FEAST* THIS RECIPE FEATURED IN HAS THE BEST FISHING SEGMENT EVER FILMED! WE WERE IN THE MIDDLE OF THE DEEPEST SEA IN THE WORLD WITH A SINGLE FISHERMAN ON A TINY BOAT WITH NO LAND IN SIGHT, PULLING IN A 30 KILOGRAM (70 POUND) TUNA ... ON A HANDLINE! WE BOUGHT IT FOR $30 AND FAUSI, OUR SHIP'S COOK, TAUGHT ME HOW TO MAKE TUNA CURRY INDONESIAN-STYLE.

SERVES 8

375 ml (13 fl oz/1½ cups) palm oil (see glossary)
2 tablespoons curry powder blend
2 salam leaves (see glossary) or bay leaves
2 kg (4 lb 6 oz) fresh tuna, diced
500 ml (17 fl oz/2 cups) coconut cream
salt and ground black pepper, to taste

PASTE
10 candlenuts (see glossary)
8 French shallots
6 red bird's eye chillies
6 garlic cloves
3 cm (1¼ inch) piece of turmeric, peeled
3 cm (1¼ inch) piece of galangal, peeled
1 stick lemongrass, smashed and left whole

To make the paste, place all of the ingredients in a spice grinder or small food processor and blend to a smooth paste.

Heat the oil in a wok over high heat, add the paste and cook for about 5 minutes or until fragrant. Stir in the curry powder and salam leaves, then add the tuna and gently stir, making sure the tuna doesn't break up.

Add the coconut cream, Season with salt and pepper, bring to the boil, then reduce the heat to low and simmer for 5 minutes. Remove from the heat and stand for 30 minutes before serving.

OKRA CURRY

IF YOU DON'T LIKE OKRA BECAUSE IT CAN BE SLIMY, TRY THIS CURRY AND YOU WILL BE CONVERTED. WHEN I WENT SHOPPING WITH MY AUNTIES AT THE FRESH VEGETABLE MARKETS IN COLOMBO, SRI LANKA, THEY ALWAYS HAD SOME GOOD ADVICE ON CHOOSING THE BEST PRODUCE. WHEN IT CAME TO OKRA, APPARENTLY IF THE OKRA IS TWISTED, IT CONTAINS A WORM, SO YOU SHOULD ONLY EVER CHOOSE OKRA THAT IS STRAIGHT.

SERVES 6

300 g (10 ½ oz) okra, trimmed and sliced
   on an angle
2 small green chillies, chopped
1 sprig curry leaves, leaves picked
1 teaspoon salt
1 teaspoon ground turmeric
½ teaspoon ground coriander
½ teaspoon ground cumin
½ teaspoon toasted and ground fennel seeds
½ teaspoon red chilli powder
½ cinnamon stick
½ teaspoon Maldive fish flakes (see glossary)
1 tablespoon vegetable oil
1 onion, chopped
300 ml (10 fl oz) coconut milk

Combine the okra, chilli, curry leaves, spices and fish flakes in a bowl and mix together well.

Heat the oil in a frying pan over medium heat, add the onion and cook until golden. Add the okra mixture and cook for 2–3 minutes or until tender.

Add the coconut milk and cook for 2 minutes.

Note *If you prefer not to have the okra so slimy, first mix the okra with the ground turmeric and fry until crisp, then continue with the recipe.*

From left to right: carrot sambal (see page 177),
coconut roti (see page 200) and tea country
pork curry (see page 68).

TEA COUNTRY PORK CURRY WITH COCONUT ROTI

THIS IS A CLASSIC TEA COUNTRY DISH OF SRI LANKA. THE LOCAL WILD BOAR LOVE EATING THE ROOTS OF THE TEA PLANTS, WHICH FLAVOURS THE MEAT AND IS WHY BOAR IS SO POPULAR AMONG THE LOCALS. IT WAS ALWAYS EXCITING WHEN ONE OF OUR RELATIVES FROM THE TEA COUNTRY CAME TO COLOMBO TO VISIT AS WE KNEW THEY WOULD BRING A PIECE OF WILD BOAR WITH THEM. DURING THE FILMING OF *MY SRI LANKA*, I WANTED TO SHOWCASE THIS DISH. AFTER THE WAR THE USE OF GUNS WAS BANNED, SO THE LOCALS CAME UP WITH AN ALTERNATIVE METHOD TO HUNT AND CATCH THE PIGS. AS THERE WERE A STILL LOT OF UNUSED MINES AND GRENADES LYING AROUND, THEY USED TO RIG THEIR HOMEMADE TRAPS WITH A GRENADE AND DISGUISE IT WITH FOOD SO THAT THE PIG WOULD TUG ON IT. YOU CAN IMAGINE WHAT HAPPENED TO THE UNFORTUNATE PIG. THIS DISH WORKS SUPERBLY WITH PORK.

SERVES 6 (PICTURED PAGE 67)

1 kg (2 lb 3 oz) pork shoulder, cubed
3 teaspoons cracked black pepper
1 teaspoon red chilli powder
4 pieces goroka (see glossary)
8 cardamom pods, cracked
¼ teaspoon fenugreek seeds
1 teaspoon roasted curry powder
1 teaspoon salt
1 cinnamon stick, broken up
¼ cup chilli flakes
juice of 2 limes
50 g (1¾ oz) ghee (see glossary)
1 sprig curry leaves, leaves picked
1 pandan leaf (see glossary), roughly torn
4 small green chillies, chopped
3 cm (1¼ inch) piece of ginger, roughly chopped
1 onion, sliced
4 garlic cloves, minced
1 litre (34 fl oz/4 cups) water or enough to cover
carrot sambal (see page 177), to serve
coconut roti (see page 200), to serve

Place the pork, pepper, chilli powder, goroka, cardamom pods, fenugreek, curry powder, salt, cinnamon, chilli flakes and lime juice in a large bowl, and, using your hands, massage the spices into the pork. Set aside for 30 minutes in the refrigerator to marinate.

Heat the ghee in a large saucepan over high heat, add the curry leaves and pandan leaf and cook until fragrant. Add the green chilli, ginger, onion and garlic and cook, stirring occasionally, until the onion is softened and translucent.

Add the pork and enough water to cover, bring to the boil, then reduce the heat to a simmer and cook for 35 minutes or until the pork is tender and cooked through.

Serve the curry with the carrot sambal and roti.

BEETROOT CURRY

VIBRANT AND TASTY, I LOVE THIS CURRY. IT IS NOT ONLY COLOURFUL BUT IT IS ALSO SO DELICIOUS IT WILL EVEN PLEASE BEETROOT HATERS. AN OLD WIVES' TALES IS THAT YOU CANNOT EAT THE LEAVES OF BEETROOT, BUT THIS IS INCORRECT, AND THESE DAYS YOU WILL FIND BABY BEETROOT LEAVES IN READY-MADE SALAD MIXES.

SERVES 6

500 g (1 lb 2 oz) beetroot (beets), tops removed, peeled and cubed
1 small green chilli, chopped
5 cm (2 inch) piece of pandan leaf (see glossary)
1 sprig curry leaves, leaves picked
1 cinnamon stick, broken up
1 teaspoon red chilli powder
1 teaspoon ground coriander
1 teaspoon salt
40 g (1½ oz) ghee (see glossary)
1 large red onion, finely chopped
2 garlic cloves, finely chopped
1 teaspoon white sugar
3 teaspoons white vinegar
300 ml (10 fl oz) coconut milk
100 ml (3½ fl oz) coconut cream, plus extra to serve

Place the beetroot, green chilli, pandan leaf, curry leaves, cinnamon, chilli powder, coriander and salt in a bowl and set aside.

Heat the ghee in a large saucepan over medium heat, add the onion and garlic and cook, stirring occasionally, until soft and translucent.

Add the beetroot mixture, sugar and vinegar and stir to combine. Add the coconut milk and cook for 15–20 minutes or until the beetroot is cooked and the sauce has reduced. To test if the curry is ready, stick a knife through a piece of beetroot; it should fall apart quite easily but still have a slight crunch to it. Taste the curry; if it is too vinegary, add a bit more sugar to balance it.

Add the coconut cream, stir to combine and cook for about 5 minutes or until the sauce is thick and glossy.

Remove from the heat and serve with a little extra coconut cream drizzled over the top.

KING'S CHICKEN CURRY

THIS DISH WAS INVENTED FOR KASYAPA, THE KING OF SIGIRIYA ROCK FORTRESS IN SRI LANKA. ACCORDING TO LEGEND, KASYAPA WAS VERY DEMANDING AND HIS CHEFS HAD TO INVENT NEW CURRIES DAILY.

SERVES 6

1 large wild fowl or chicken (about 1.6 kg/3lb 8 oz)
100 g (3½ oz) brown onions, thinly sliced
4 garlic cloves
2 pieces of pandan leaf (see glossary), roughly torn
1 sprig curry leaves, leaves picked
2 long red chillies, chopped
4 small green chillies, chopped
2 teaspoons ground brown mustard seeds
10 black peppercorns
salt, to taste
3 cm (1¼ inch) piece of turmeric, peeled
½ teaspoon brown mustard seeds
90 ml (3 fl oz) vegetable oil
2 tablespoons white vinegar
10 cm (4 inch) piece of sandalwood (see note)
6 whole cloves
4 cardamom pods, cracked
½ teaspoon dark roasted curry powder
1 tablespoon red chilli powder
80 ml (3 fl oz) malt vinegar
1 stick lemongrass
1 cinnamon stick
¼ teaspoon fenugreek seeds, toasted
500 ml (17 fl oz/2 cups) water, or enough to cover
500 ml (17 fl oz/2 cups) coconut cream
juice of 2 limes
10 dried red chillies, quickly fried until crisp, to garnish

Cut the chicken into six pieces. Place in a large bowl with the onion, garlic, pandan leaf, curry leaves, and red and green chilli, and and toss to coat the chicken. Add the ground mustard seeds and peppercorns and season with salt. Massage the mixture into the chicken and marinate for at least 20 minutes.

Meanwhile, using a mortar and pestle, crush the turmeric with the mustard seeds to form a paste. Set aside.

Heat 2 tablespoons of the oil in a large frying pan over medium heat. Remove the chicken from the spice marinade, reserving the marinade. Once the oil is hot, place the chicken, skin side down, in the pan and cook until the skin is crisp. Turn the chicken over and cook the other side. Remove from the heat and set aside.

Meanwhile, heat 50 ml (1¾ fl oz) of the oil in another large saucepan over medium heat, add the reserved spice marinade and the sandalwood and fry until fragrant. Add the cloves and cardamom and fry for 3 minutes.

Add the turmeric paste, curry powder and chilli powder and season with salt and pepper. Add the vinegar and scrape the base of the pan with a wooden spatula to remove any stuck-on spices.

Add the chicken, lemongrass, cinnamon, fenugreek and enough water to just cover the chicken and gently simmer for 45 minutes to 1 hour or until the chicken is cooked through, topping up the water as necessary to ensure the water level doesn't drop too much.

Once cooked, add the coconut cream and bring to the boil, then immediately remove from the heat and stir in the lime juice.

To serve, remove the chicken from the pan and pile high on a plate. Garnish with the fried dried red chillies.

Note *Fresh sandalwood is very expensive and difficult to find. If you want an authentic flavour, I suggest you substitute with a few drops of pure sandalwood oil added with the water. It will produce a similar result.*

SNAKE BEAN CURRY

SNAKE BEANS ARE CALLED *MAAKAREL* IN SINHALESE. I WAS ALWAYS TAUGHT TO LOOK FOR BEANS THAT ARE BRIGHTLY COLOURED AND ONES THAT SNAP WHEN YOU BREAK THEM IN HALF. MAKE SURE YOU DON'T OVERCOOK THE BEANS, THAT WAY THEY WILL REMAIN A VIBRANT GREEN. THIS CURRY SHOULD BE FAIRLY DRY, SO MAKE SURE YOU STIR IT CONSTANTLY SO NONE OF THE SPICES BURN, ESPECIALLY THE FENUGREEK, OTHERWISE IT WILL ADD A BITTERNESS TO THE CURRY THAT WILL RUIN ITS TASTE.

SERVES 6

350 g (12 oz) snake (yard-long) beans,
   trimmed and broken into small pieces
1 teaspoon chilli flakes
½ teaspoon fennel seeds
¼ teaspoon ground turmeric
½ teaspoon fenugreek seeds
1 teaspoon ground cumin
salt, to taste
1 small onion, finely chopped
2 garlic cloves, chopped
2 small green chillies, finely chopped
2 tablespoons vegetable oil
1 sprig curry leaves, leaves picked
125 ml (4 fl oz / ½ cup) coconut cream

Place the snake beans in a bowl with the chilli flakes, coriander, fennel seeds, turmeric, fenugreek and cumin, season with salt and toss to coat the beans. Add the onion, garlic and green chilli.

Heat the oil in a saucepan over high heat, add the curry leaves and cook until they start to sizzle. Add the snake bean mixture and cook, stirring constantly, until the mixture starts to caramelise and the beans are just cooked, making sure the spices don't burn.

Add the coconut cream, stir to combine and cook for a few minutes or until the beans are cooked through. Cover with a lid until ready to serve.

LOTUS ROOT CURRY

YALA NATIONAL PARK IN THE SOUTH-EAST OF SRI LANKA HAS ABUNDANT WILDLIFE. WE FILMED A SEGMENT THERE WITH A SHAMAN WHO HELPED US FORAGE FOR LOCAL BUSH FOOD. THIS LED US THROUGH A WILD BUFFALO-INFESTED SWAMP TO A BEAUTIFUL LAKE COVERED IN LOTUS — IT WAS A BEAUTIFUL SEA OF YELLOW AND PURPLE FLOWERS. WE WADED THROUGH THE LAKE AND HE TAUGHT ME HOW TO HARVEST THE ROOTS OF THE LOTUS, AS WELL AS HOW TO EAT THE SEEDS FROM INSIDE THE FLOWERS AND THE TASTY BULB AT THE BASE. AFTER PREPARING THIS CURRY WE SAT DOWN TO EAT IT IN A BUSH CAMP, WHICH FRONTED THE OCEAN. AS WE SAT AND CHATTED A SMALL HERD OF WILD ELEPHANTS WANDERED PAST US ON THE BEACH. IT WAS QUITE A SIGHT AND A MEMORABLE MEAL OF SRI LANKAN BUSH FOOD.

SERVES 6

225 g (8 oz) lotus root, cut into 2 cm (¾ inch) pieces
2 tomatoes, sliced
1 small green chilli, sliced
1 sprig curry leaves, leaves picked
½ teaspoon fenugreek seeds
½ teaspoon salt
250 ml (8½ fl oz/1 cup) thick coconut milk
¼ teaspoon ground turmeric
½ teaspoon red chilli powder
25 g (⅞ oz) ghee (see glossary)
1 large French shallot, sliced
1 teaspoon roasted curry powder

Place the lotus root, tomato, green chilli, curry leaves, fenugreek, salt, coconut milk, turmeric and chilli powder in a saucepan and cook over medium heat for about 10 minutes or until the lotus root is cooked.

Heat the ghee in a small frying pan over medium heat. When sizzling, add the eschalot and cook until soft and translucent.

Add to the lotus root mixture along with the curry powder, stir to combine and cook for about 1 minute.

BREADFRUIT CURRY

WHEN I LIVED IN VATULELE IN FIJI THERE WERE BREADFRUIT TREES ALL OVER MY NEIGHBOURHOOD. I USED TO WATCH THE BREADFRUITS MATURE ON THE TREES, WAITING FOR WHEN THEY WERE PERFECTLY RIPE, BUT THE NIGHT BEFORE I WAS READY TO PICK THEM, THEY WOULD DISAPPEAR. OBVIOUSLY I WAS NOT THE ONLY ONE WATCHING THE FRUIT RIPEN. AFTER A FEW MONTHS OF CONSTANTLY MISSING OUT, I DECIDED TO WRITE MY NAME ON A RIPENING BREADFRUIT THAT I HAD MY EYE ON. IT WORKED. WHEN THE DAY CAME FOR THE FRUIT TO BE PICKED, THE LOCALS CAME AND TOLD ME IT WAS READY. UNFORTUNATELY, BREADFRUIT IS DIFFICULT TO FIND IN MOST WESTERN COUNTRIES. IT IS AVAILABLE FROZEN OR TINNED. THE TINNED VERSION WORKS WELL IN THIS CURRY, WHICH MAKES THE MOST OF THE FRUIT'S CREAMY TEXTURE AND FLAVOUR.

SERVES 6

1 teaspoon ground coriander
1 teaspoon ground cumin
1 teaspoon vegetable curry powder (see glossary)
1 breadfruit (about 500 g/1 lb 2 oz), peeled and cut into 3 cm (1¼ inch) pieces
100 g (3½ oz) onion, finely chopped
3 garlic cloves, chopped
2 small green chillies, halved lengthways
1 sprig curry leaves, leaves picked
3 cm (1¼ inch) piece of cinnamon stick
4 cm (1½ inch) piece of pandan leaf (see glossary), roughly torn
½ teaspoon ground turmeric
½ teaspoon ground black pepper
1 teaspoon brown mustard seeds (see glossary), finely ground
salt, to taste
500 ml (17 fl oz/2 cups) coconut milk
100 ml (3½ fl oz) coconut cream
pinch of dark roasted curry powder

TEMPERING
100 ml (3½ fl oz) vegetable oil
1 teaspoon brown mustard seeds
1 sprig curry leaves, leaves picked
½ red onion, finely chopped

Place the coriander, cumin and vegetable curry powder in a small heavy-based frying pan over low heat and roast until dark brown.

Place the toasted spices and the remaining ingredients, except the coconut cream and dark toasted curry powder, in a heavy-based saucepan over medium heat and simmer for 12 minutes or until the breadfruit is tender.

To make the tempering, heat the oil in a small frying pan over medium–high heat, add the mustard seeds and curry leaves and cook until the mustards seeds pop. Add the onion and cook until soft and translucent.

Add the tempered mix to the breadfruit mixture and stir to combine.

While stirring constantly, add the coconut cream and cook for 4 minutes or until just below boiling point. Do not boil. The sauce should be thick and the breadfruit soft and tender. Season with salt.

To serve, transfer to a serving dish and sprinkle with the dark toasted curry powder — do not stir it in.

SOUTHERN DRY FISH CURRY
AMBUL THIAL

THIS IS A FAVOURITE IN SRI LANKA. THE COOKING METHOD WAS USED TO PRESERVE FISH IN THE DAYS OF NO REFRIGERATION. IT IS A WONDERFUL AND TASTY WAY TO PREPARE TUNA OR OTHER OILY FISH. THERE ARE MANY VERSIONS BUT THE MOST IMPORTANT INGREDIENTS ARE GOROKA, BLACK PEPPER, CHILLI AND LIME AND THE TUNA WILL ADD ITS OWN FLAVOUR ONCE IT HAS BEEN COOKED. MY RECIPE IS MORE COMPLEX AND HAS BEEN PULLED STRAIGHT FROM MY FAMILY KITCHEN.

SERVES 6

450 g (1 lb) tuna steak, cut into 3 cm (1¼ inch) pieces
juice of 1 lime
5 pieces goroka (see glossary), soaked in warm water
   for 30 minutes
6 garlic cloves, minced
2 cm (¾ inch) piece of ginger, coarsely chopped
1 tablespoon red chilli powder
2 teaspoons ground black pepper
1 teaspoon salt
1 teaspoon ground coriander
½ teaspoon ground cumin
½ teaspoon roasted Sri Lankan curry powder
   (see glossary)
2 green cardamom pods, seeds removed
1 cinnamon stick
2 sprigs curry leaves, leaves picked
2 small green chillies, halved lengthways
250 ml (8½ fl oz/1 cup) water

Combine the tuna and lime juice in a bowl and leave for 5 minutes, drain, then place the tuna in a single layer in a large heavy-based saucepan.

Drain the goroka, place in a mortar and pestle with the garlic, ginger and all of the spices, except the cinnamon, and pound until a paste forms.

Combine the paste with the cinnamon, curry leaves, chilli and water and pour over the tuna and combine well.

Bring to the boil over medium–low heat, then reduce the heat to a gentle simmer and cook for 5 minutes or until most of the liquid has evaporated.

THAI EGGPLANT COCONUT CURRY

YOU PROBABLY WALK PAST THESE EGGPLANTS, WHICH LOOK LIKE PERFECT GREEN BALLS, IN THE VEGETABLE SECTION AND WONDER WHAT TO DO WITH THEM. WELL HERE IS AN EASY AND TASTY WHOLESOME VEGETARIAN DISH THAT WILL PLEASE THE FUSSIEST HERBIVORE. THIS CURRY IS A CHILDHOOD FAVOURITE. I RANG MY COUSIN TO GET THE RECIPE AND SHE GAVE ME THE FOLLOWING. AS WITH MOST SRI LANKAN CURRIES, EACH HOUSEHOLD WILL MAKE IT SLIGHTLY DIFFERENTLY. THIS IS THE DEHIWALA KURUVITA VERSION.

SERVES 6

900 g (2 lb) Thai eggplants
50 ml (1¾ fl oz) vegetable oil
¼ teaspoon brown mustard seeds
½ onion, chopped
1 sprig curry leaves, leaves picked
1 garlic clove, chopped
1 small green chilli, chopped
2 teaspoons Sri Lankan curry powder (see glossary)
1 teaspoon ground turmeric
1 teaspoon Maldive fish flakes (see glossary)
300 ml (10 fl oz) water
250 ml (8½ fl oz/1 cup) coconut cream
juice of ½ lime
salt, to taste

To prepare the eggplants, place them in a plastic bag and gently tap them until they all split open. Remove from the bag and pull out all the seeds and stems. Cut the eggplants into even strips, rinse in cold water and set aside.

Heat the oil in a heavy-based saucepan over medium heat, add the mustard seeds and cook until they start to pop. Add the onion and curry leaves and cook until the onion starts to turn brown.

Add the eggplant, garlic, chilli, curry powder, turmeric and fish flakes, and stir to combine. Add the water, bring to the boil, then reduce the heat to a simmer and cook for about 5 minutes or until the eggplant is soft.

Add the coconut cream and bring to the boil, then immediately remove from the heat. Finish with the lime juice and season with salt.

BITTER GOURD CURRY

BITTER GOURD IS, AS ITS NAME SUGGESTS, VERY BITTER AND AN ACQUIRED TASTE BUT, AS WITH MOST FOODS USED IN SRI LANKAN COOKING, IT HAS TREMENDOUS HEALTH BENEFITS. UNFORTUNATELY, TO GET THE BEST OUT OF THIS VEGETABLE, IT IS SAID THE GREENER (AND HENCE MORE BITTER) THE GOURD, THE MORE BENEFITS IT CONTAINS. IF YOU WANT TO USE IT MEDICINALLY I WOULD SUGGEST YOU JUICE ONE OF THESE KNOBBY VEGETABLES, PINCH YOUR NOSE AND THROW IT DOWN. AS KIDS IN SRI LANKA, WE USED TO PLAY A TASTE-TEST GAME TO SEE WHO COULD TOLERATE EATING THE GOURD.

SERVES 6

2 bitter gourds, halved, seeds removed and thinly sliced
1 tablespoon salt
100 ml (3½ fl oz) vegetable oil
½ onion, finely chopped
½ teaspoon brown mustard seeds
1 teaspoon ground cumin seeds
½ tablespoon ground turmeric
1 teaspoon red chilli powder
½ tomato, chopped
60 ml (2 fl oz/3 tablespoons) water
125 ml (4 fl oz/½ cup) coconut milk
juice of ½ lime or lemon

Sprinkle the gourd with the salt and set aside for 10 minutes, then rinse in water, drain and squeeze out the excess water. Set aside.

Heat the oil in a frying pan over medium heat, add the onion and mustard seeds and cook until the mustard seeds begin to pop.

Add the cumin, turmeric and chilli powder, stir for a few seconds, then add the gourd and stir to combine.

Add the tomato, water and coconut milk, season with salt and cook, stirring occasionally for 5 minutes or until the gourd is soft.

Stir in the lime juice and check the taste – the lime offsets the bitterness of the gourd.

CASHEW NUT CURRY

WE ARRIVED IN SRI LANKA TO BEGIN FILMING *MY SRI LANKA* A DAY BEFORE ONE OF THE BIGGEST FESTIVALS IN THE COLOMBO AREA, THE *KELANIYA PERAHERA*, A PROCESSION WITH NO LESS THAN THIRTY ELEPHANTS DRESSED IN ALL THEIR FINERY. IT'S A VERY EXCITING SPECTACLE AND I SHARED WITH THE CREW MY MEMORIES AS A KID IN THE THRONG OF 100,000 PEOPLE WATCHING THE PARADE. THE BUILD-UP WAS AMAZING, WITH PEOPLE WALKING AROUND A GIANT BODHI TREE PLANTED FROM A SEEDLING FROM THE ORIGINAL TREE UNDER WHICH LORD BUDDHA IS SAID TO HAVE FOUND ENLIGHTENMENT.

OUR DRIVER FOUND A PARKING SPOT FOR US IN THE TEMPLE GROUNDS AND WE WENT TO WORK TO PREPARE A MEAL FOR FILMING. I COOKED THIS LUSCIOUS AND REGAL CURRY AS A THANK YOU TO THE HIGH PRIEST OF THE TEMPLE.

SERVES 6

250 g (9 oz) raw unsalted cashew nuts
40 g (1½ oz) ghee (see glossary)
1 large onion, finely chopped
1 sprig curry leaves, leaves picked
2 small green chillies, chopped
10 cm (4 inch) piece of pandan leaf (see glossary)
½ teaspoon cumin seeds, toasted and ground
½ teaspoon ground turmeric
1 teaspoon red chilli powder
1 cinnamon stick
300 ml (10 fl oz) coconut milk
150 ml (5 fl oz) coconut cream, plus extra to serve
salt, to taste
pinch of roasted curry powder

Soak the cashew nuts in a small bowl of water for 1 hour. Once softened, drain and set aside to dry off a bit.

Meanwhile, heat the ghee in a medium saucepan over high heat. Once hot, add the onion, curry leaves, green chilli and pandan leaf and cook until the onion is fragrant and is starting to change colour.

Add the cumin, turmeric, chilli powder and cinnamon stick and stir over medium heat until the spices are lightly toasted. Add the nuts and stir to combine. Add the coconut milk, bring to the boil and cook until the sauce has thickened and reduced by half.

Stir in the coconut cream, bring to the boil, then remove from the heat and season with salt.

Serve topped with a little extra coconut cream and the roasted curry powder.

Jaffna goat curry

Jaffna and goat go hand in hand. Goat is a staple in the diet of this region in the north of Sri Lanka. Choose a cut of goat which is low in fat but with the bones in so that the sauce sticks to every morsel. This dish was finished with the liver and heart of the goat that we butchered in the village, but it works just as well without the addition of the offal; you can substitute it with tomato paste. You can also replace the goat with lamb.

SERVES 6

400 g (14 oz) goat, preferably chump chops with bones
1 litre (34 fl oz/4 cups) water
100 g (3½ oz) onion, diced
1 sprig curry leaves, leaves picked
1 cinnamon stick
2 garlic cloves
2 thin slices ginger
10 cm (4 inch) piece of pandan leaf
10 cm (4 inch) piece of lemongrass
7 cardamom pods, cracked
2 tablespoons tomato paste (concentrated purée)
2 teaspoons ground coriander, toasted
1 teaspoon dark roasted curry powder
1 teaspoon Jaffna curry powder (see glossary)
1 teaspoon ground cumin, toasted
½ teaspoon fenugreek seeds, lightly toasted
½ teaspoon red chilli powder
½ teaspoon ground turmeric
juice of ½ lime

Chop the goat into 2 cm (¾ inch) pieces with the bone in. Place all of the ingredients in a heavy-based saucepan and bring to the boil, then reduce the heat to a simmer and cook for 25 minutes or until the gravy thickens and the goat is tender.

YAM CURRY

WHILE FORAGING IN THE JUNGLE IN SRI LANKA, WE SAW THIS UNIQUE POTATO. A THIN VINE GREW FROM THE GROUND AND I LEARNED THAT WHEN IT BORE FRUIT, IT MEANT THAT THE YAM BELOW GROUND WAS READY TO BE HARVESTED. WE DUG UP THE YAM AND WHEN PEELED IT WAS REALLY SLIMY, BUT ONCE COOKED IT WAS FLUFFY AND SOFT — IT HAD A SLIGHTLY NUTTY FLAVOUR AND A SMOOTH TEXTURE.

SERVES 6

1 large Sri Lankan yam or white sweet potato, peeled and
    cut into 2 cm (¾ inch) thick pieces
salt, to taste
freshly grated coconut, to serve

Place the yam and salt in a large saucepan and add enough water to cover. Cover, bring to the boil over high heat and continue to cook for 15–20 minutes or until the yam is cooked through.

Drain the yam and return to the pan, cover with the lid and leave for 5 minutes or until the yam has fluffed up.

Garnish with the coconut to serve.

SQUID CURRY

THIS IS A FAMILY FAVOURITE AND A REAL SOUTHERN SRI LANKAN DISH. SQUID IS PLENTIFUL ALL OVER THE WORLD AND THE SECRET OF COOKING SQUID PERFECTLY IS NOT TO OVERCOOK IT. I AM HAPPY NOT TO CLEAN THE SQUID COMPLETELY. SIMPLY REMOVE THE HEAD, CUT OUT THE BEAK AND REMOVE THE INNARDS — THE REST IS EDIBLE.

SERVES 6

350 g (12 oz) squid, cleaned, heads cut into
   1 cm (3/8 inch) thick rings and tentacles reserved
3 pieces goroka (see glossary)
1½ teaspoons ground coriander
1 teaspoon ground cumin
½ teaspoon red chilli powder
½ teaspoon ground turmeric
¼ teaspoon fennel seeds
¼ teaspoon fenugreek seeds
½ teaspoon ground black pepper
50 g (1¾ oz) ghee (see glossary)
½ onion, finely chopped
3 garlic cloves, thinly sliced
1 sprig curry leaves, leaves picked
2 small green chillies, chopped
300 ml (10 fl oz) coconut milk
100 ml (3½ fl oz) coconut cream
juice of ½ lime
salt, to taste

Place the squid rings and tentacles, goroka and all of the spices in a bowl and combine well.

Heat the ghee in a heavy-based saucepan over medium heat, add the onion, garlic, curry leaves and green chilli and cook, stirring regularly, for 4 minutes or until the onion is golden.

Increase the heat to high, add the squid and stir for 3 minutes.

Add the coconut milk, reduce the heat to low and simmer for 10 minutes or until the squid is tender.

Stir in the coconut cream and lime juice and season with salt. The sauce should be thick and dark.

TEMPERED RADISH RAABU

THIS IS ONE OF THE MORE DISTINCTIVE VEGETABLE CURRIES. IT IS VERY TASTY AND GOES WELL WITH A FISH CURRY.

SERVES 6

1 tablespoon vegetable oil
1 onion, sliced
1 sprig curry leaves, leaves picked
2 small green chillies, sliced
450 g (1 lb) red radish, peeled and grated
1–2 teaspoons lime juice
1 teaspoon ground coriander
½ teaspoon ground cumin
2 teaspoons red chilli powder
2 teaspoons Maldive fish flakes (see glossary)
   (optional)
1 teaspoon chilli flakes
¼ teaspoon ground turmeric
salt, to taste
150 ml (5 fl oz) coconut milk

Heat the oil in a frying pan over medium heat, then add the onion, curry leaves and green chilli and cook until the onion is golden.

Add the radish, lime juice, coriander, cumin, chilli powder, fish flakes, chilli flakes and turmeric, season with salt and stir well. Cook for 2–3 minutes over high heat, then reduce the heat to low and cook until the radish is tender.

Stir through the coconut milk towards the end.

MAHI MAHI CURRY WITH SAVOURY ROLLS

THIS IS WHAT I CALL MODERN SRI LANKAN CUISINE. I SERVE THIS AT MY RESTAURANTS FLYING FISH FIJI AND FLYING FISH SYDNEY. IT HAS BEEN A WINNER FROM DAY ONE. IT'S A MORE ELEGANT WAY TO SERVE CURRY.

SERVES 6

2 tablespoons vegetable oil
6 x 180 g (6½ oz) portions mahi mahi or
   snapper fillets, skin on
salt, to taste
prawn and sweet potato rolls (see page 16), to serve
tomato sambal (see page 177), to serve

MAHI MAHI CURRY

50 ml (1¾ fl oz) vegetable oil
1 onion, roughly chopped
2 garlic cloves, roughly chopped
5 cm (2 inch) piece of pandan leaf, roughly torn
2 sprigs curry leaves
2 small green chillies, halved lengthways
½ teaspoon fenugreek seeds
½ teaspoon fennel seeds
1 teaspoon red chilli powder
2 teaspoons ground cumin
1 teaspoon ground coriander
1 teaspoon ground turmeric
1 cinnamon stick, broken into pieces
3 pieces goroka (see glossary)
500 ml (17 fl oz/2 cups) coconut milk
1 kg (2 lb 3 oz) fish bones

To make the mahi mahi curry, heat the oil in a large saucepan over medium heat, add the onion, garlic, pandan leaf, curry leaves and green chilli and cook until the onion is soft and translucent. Add all of the spices, the goroka, coconut milk and fish bones, stir to combine and cook until the mixture has reduced by half. Strain the curry through a fine mesh sieve into a bowl, discarding the solids. Set the curry aside.

Heat the oil in a saucepan over high heat, season the pan with salt, gently place the fish, skin side down, and cook for a few minutes or until the skin is crispy. Turn the fish and cook the other side. Remove from the heat.

To serve, place a piece of fish, skin side up, on each plate, drizzle with the curry and serve with the prawn and sweet potato rolls and tomato sambal.

PUMPKIN CURRY WITH EGGPLANT ROTI TRIANGLES

I COOKED THIS DISH IN A BEAUTIFUL HOTEL IN KANDY, FOR MY TELEVISION SERIES *MY SRI LANKA*. WHILE FILMING, I RECEIVED NEWS THAT MY UNCLE ROY HAD PASSED AWAY. HE WAS A VERY GOOD FRIEND OF THE FAMILY. HE AND HIS WIFE LYN MET MY PARENTS IN LONDON LONG BEFORE WE WERE BORN AND THEY REMAINED CLOSE FRIENDS EVER SINCE. WHEN WE LIVED IN SRI LANKA, OUR FAMILIES USED TO POST EACH OTHER TAPES OF THE KIDS — THESE WERE THE OLD REEL-TO-REEL TAPES, AND DELIVERY TIME WAS ABOUT TWO TO THREE MONTHS. THE ONLY SRI LANKAN THING I REMEMBERED ABOUT HIM WAS HIS LOVE OF AN OLD BILA TUNE IN SINHALESE CALLED *BABI ACHIS BICYCLEL ECK A*. FOR FILMING, WE HAD ORGANISED A CALYPSO BAND FOR THE LAST SHOT OF THE SEGMENT, AND AFTER FILMING, I ASKED THEM TO PLAY HIS FAVOURITE TUNE IN MEMORY OF HIM. IT WAS BEAUTIFUL.

SERVES 6

1 teaspoon long-grain rice
2 tablespoons freshly grated or desiccated coconut
1 large onion, finely chopped
1 sprig curry leaves, leaves picked
100 ml (3½ fl oz) coconut cream
1 teaspoon hot English mustard
500 g (1 lb 2 oz) Jap or Kent pumpkin, seeds removed and cut into 3 cm (1¼ inch) thick x 5 cm (2 inch) diameter circles
2 small green chillies
1 teaspoon Maldive fish flakes (see glossary)
2 garlic cloves, thinly sliced
¼ teaspoon ground turmeric
1 teaspoon ground cumin
1 teaspoon ground coriander
300 ml (10 fl oz) coconut milk
salt, to taste
pinch of dark roasted curry powder
eggplant roti triangles (see page 201), to serve

Place the rice in a dry frying pan and stir over medium heat until it is light golden brown, then remove from the pan.

To the same pan, add the coconut, onion and curry leaves and stir for 5 minutes or until the coconut turns dark brown.

Place the roasted rice and coconut mixture in a mortar and pestle and pound until a paste forms. Add the coconut cream and mustard and combine well.

Place the pumpkin, chilli, fish flakes, garlic, turmeric, cumin, coriander and coconut mixture in a saucepan and bring to the boil.

Reduce the heat to medium and simmer until the pumpkin is tender.

While stirring constantly, add the coconut milk and bring to just below the boil. Remove from the heat, season with salt, then sprinkle with a little curry powder and serve with eggplant roti triangles.

Meat and Poultry

TARTLET OF BRAISED OXTAIL WITH PEARS AND BITTER CHOCOLATE

COCOA WAS ONE OF THE DISCOVERIES COLUMBUS MADE WHILE SEARCHING THE SPICE ROUTES IN THE EAST. THIS IS AN ELEGANT DISH OF CHOCOLATE COMBINED WITH DARK BEER AND OXTAIL. RICH AND HEARTY, THESE TARTLETS CAN BE EITHER A CANAPÉ OR STARTER.

MAKES 12

2 large red radishes
2 tablespoons lemon juice
vegetable oil, for cooking
2 x 500 g (1 lb 2 oz) oxtails, trimmed and
    cut into 4 equal-sized pieces
salt, to taste
1 onion, sliced
1 garlic clove, sliced
125 ml (4 fl oz/½ cup) port
juice and finely grated zest of 1 orange
500 ml (17 fl oz/2 cups) beef stock
500 ml (17 fl oz/2 cups) porter or other dark beer
1 tablespoon cracked black pepper
50 g (1¾ oz) butter, diced
60 g (2 oz) dark chocolate (70% cocoa solids),
    broken up
12 savoury tartlet shells (3 cm/1¼ inches in diameter)
baby herbs, to garnish

CAULIFLOWER PURÉE

30 ml (1 fl oz) vegetable oil
5 French shallots, finely chopped
3 garlic cloves, finely chopped
1 head cauliflower, chopped
500 ml (17 fl oz/2 cups) chicken stock
salt and ground black pepper, to taste

To make the cauliflower purée, heat the oil in a large frying pan over medium heat, add the shallot and garlic and cook until soft but not coloured. Add the cauliflower and stock and cook until the cauliflower has softened and is breaking apart. Strain and reserve the liquid. Purée the solids until smooth, thinning with some of the reserved liquid if necessary. Season with salt and pepper. Set aside and keep warm.

Peel and thinly slice the radishes. Cover with the lemon juice and a little water and set aside until needed.

Preheat the oven to 180°C (360°F/Gas 4).

Heat a little bit of oil in a large ovenproof frying pan over high heat, season the oxtail with salt, add to the pan and cook until browned on all sides. Remove from the pan and set aside.

Add the onion and garlic to the same pan and cook over medium heat until brown. Return the oxtail to the pan, deglaze with the port and orange juice, reduce the heat and cook until the liquid is syrupy.

Add the stock, beer, pepper and orange zest, cover with baking paper and place in the oven for about 3 hours or until the meat is very tender.

When the oxtail is cooked, remove from the pan and while still hot, remove all the meat from the bones and keep warm.

Place a sieve over a bowl and strain the cooking liquid. Pour the liquid into a clean pan and reduce to a syrupy consistency, then whisk in the butter and chocolate. Add the oxtail meat and stir to coat.

To serve, place a teaspoonful of the cauliflower purée into each tartlet shell, then the oxtail mixture and garnish with the radish and baby herbs.

Barbecued island beef with salsa verde

The beautiful charolais cattle feeding on the green pastures and coconuts on the private island of Ratua in Vanuatu inspired this dish. I had the opportunity to visit this amazing island owned by a gentleman who made a lot of money in the technology boom and bought himself a motor yacht and set out with his family to see the world. Along the way he fell in love with Indonesia and its architecture, and he also discovered Ratua Island. He bought the island, and to fulfil his love of Indonesian architecture, he bought a whole wooden village and had it rebuilt on his island. The result is beautiful. It is now a not-for-profit private resort, and open to outside guests.

SERVES 6

1 x 3 kg (6 lb 10 oz) standing beef rib roast,
  separated into fillet and sirloin
1 bunch Thai coriander (pointed cilantro),
  leaves roughly chopped
½ bunch flat-leaf (Italian) parsley, leaves roughly chopped
2 sprigs thyme, leaves roughly chopped
salt and ground black pepper, to taste
3 cobs corn, silks removed but with the husks left on
salsa verde (see page 189), to serve
sky potato salad (see page 171), to serve
bean salad (see page 170), to serve

Pull the fat away from the fillet and remove the sinew from the sirloin, then cut away the fat and the tail end of the sirloin.

Place the coriander, parsley and thyme in a flat container, season with salt and pepper, then roll the fillet over the herbs to coat. Set aside until ready to cook.

Place the corn in a large saucepan of water over high heat, bring to the boil and cook for 10 minutes or until just cooked. Drain and set aside.

Preheat a barbecue hotplate until hot. Cook the corn for 8–10 minutes, turning once.

Take some of the oil from the salsa verde and brush it onto the hottest part of the hotplate, then place the meat on top, brush with the salsa verde, season with salt and pepper and cook, turning once, for 8–10 minutes for medium-rare.

Remove the corn and meat and leave the meat to rest for a few minutes. Cut the sirloin into six portions. Serve with the potato salad and bean salad.

SLOW-COOKED TEA-INFUSED DUCK BREASTS

THIS IS AN EXAMPLE OF HOW YOU CAN COOK WITH TEA. HERE IT IS USED AS A TENDERISER AND MARINADE.

SERVES 2

2 skinless duck breasts
250 ml (8½ fl oz/1 cup) earl grey tea, strained, cooled and tea leaves reserved
300 ml (10 fl oz) apple juice
½ teaspoon coriander seeds
½ bay leaf
1 sprig thyme
2 small French shallots, sliced
60 g (2 oz/¼ cup) duck fat
100 ml (3½ fl oz) good-quality beef jus
salt and ground black pepper, to taste
250 ml (8½ fl oz/1 cup) lime and orange tea (or other similar fruit-flavoured tea), strained, cooled and tea leaves reserved

SALAD
50 ml (1¾ fl oz) olive oil
1 tablespoon orange juice
pinch of finely grated orange zest
salt and ground black pepper, to taste
1 small frisée lettuce (curly endive/chicory), torn
1 small handful baby herbs
50 g (1¾ oz) toasted walnuts
50 g (1¾ oz) green beans, cooked and cut into 5 cm (2 inch) lengths
12 black olives, halved
6 cherry tomatoes, halved

Place the duck breasts in a high-sided container with 1 teaspoon of the reserved earl grey tea leaves, the apple juice, coriander seeds, bay leaf, thyme and shallot and refrigerate for 2 hours to marinate. (Sip the earl grey tea while cooking or discard.)

Preheat the oven to 60°C (140°F) fan-forced (if your oven doesn't go down this low, leave the door ajar and monitor the temperature with an oven thermometer).

Drain the duck breasts and pat dry with paper towel. Place in an ovenproof dish, add the duck fat, beef jus, season with salt and pepper, 100 ml (3½ fl oz) of the lime and orange tea and ½ teaspoon of the tea leaves. (Discard the remaining lime and orange tea.) Ensure the duck breasts are covered by the liquid and heat on the stove to 50°C (120°F), then transfer to the oven and cook for 35 minutes.

When done, remove the duck breasts from the liquid and allow to cool.

Once cool, slice each breast diagonally into 6 slices.

To make the salad, mix the oil, orange juice and orange zest in a bowl and season with salt and pepper. Set the dressing aside. Combine the remaining ingredients in a bowl and toss together. Dress just before serving.

To serve, divide the salad between plates and top with the duck slices. Heat the cooking juices and drizzle over.

Kare kare

This dish was brought to the Philippines by Sikh soldiers in the British Army and then made into a unique and very Filipino dish. Apparently the British decided to send 500 Indian troops to the Philippines to annoy the Spaniards. Once there. the soldiers loved the place and the people, and when they were recalled they refused to go and decided to stay. The soldiers settled on the route to a pilgrimage site and each year as the pilgrims passed the soldiers offered them rice and curry. Word soon spread about these curries and in true Pinoy style the locals started making their own versions. Just like many Filipino dishes, it has morphed into the kare kare of today; a world away from the original rice and curry.

SERVES 6

4 slices eggplant (aubergine), about 2.5 cm (1 inch) thick
1 banana bud (flower), outer leaves removed, inner core cut into 2.5 cm (1 inch) thick slices
1 bunch snake (yard-long) beans, trimmed
salt, to taste
chilli paste and steamed rice, to serve

STOCK
1 kg (2 lb 3 oz) oxtail or beef (round or sirloin) or beef tripe or a combination, cut into 5 cm (2 inch) pieces
1 dried bay leaf
2 litres (4 pt 4 fl oz) water

KARE KARE SAUCE
125 ml (4 fl oz/½ cup) vegetable oil
80 ml (3 fl oz/⅓ cup) annatto oil (see glossary)
3 garlic cloves, minced
1 small onion, diced
1 tablespoon crunchy peanut butter
1 tablespoon smooth peanut butter
50 g (1¾ oz/¼ cup) ground toasted rice

To make the stock, place the oxtail, beef or tripe (or whatever meat you have chosen) in a large stockpot with the bay leaf and water, bring to the boil over high heat, then reduce the heat to low and simmer gently for 1 hour or until cooked. Strain, reserve the stock and keep the meat warm.

To make the kare kare sauce, heat both the oils in a large saucepan or wok over medium heat, add the garlic and onion and cook until golden. Add the peanut butters and 1 litre (34 fl oz/4 cups) of the reserved stock and simmer until reduced by half. Add the toasted rice and stir until thick and gelatinous. Remove from the heat and keep warm.

Grill the eggplant over an open wood fire or on a barbecue grill until the skin is charred and blackened.

Cook the banana bud and string beans in separate pans of boiling salted water until tender but still firm to the bite. Drain and keep warm.

To serve, season the meat and arrange on a plate with the vegetables. Pour the hot kare kare sauce over and serve with the chilli paste and rice.

LUMP RICE LAMPREYS

SERVES 4

5 cups uncooked rice
8 banana leaves
100 ml (3½ fl oz) coconut cream
eggplant pickle (see page 201)
12 Dutch forced meatballs (see page 40)
20 fried banana chips
10 toothpicks
tomato sambal (see page 177), to serve
sambal terasi (see page 180), to serve

MEAT CURRY

150 g (5 oz) braising beef, cut into 2 cm (¾ Inch) cubes
150 g (5 oz) skinless chicken thigh fillet,
   cut into 2 cm (¾ inch) cubes
150 g (5 oz) pork shoulder, cut into 2 cm (¾ inch) cubes
150 g (5 oz) goat or lamb leg, cut into 2 cm (¾ inch) cubes
100 g (3½ oz) ox liver, cut into 2 cm (¾ inch) cubes
2 litres (4 pt 4 fl oz) water
5 cardamom pods, cracked
1 small cinnamon stick, broken up
4 whole cloves
2 teaspoons salt
¾ teaspoon toasted and ground fennel seeds
1 teaspoon ground cumin
2 teaspoons ground coriander
1 tablespoon chilli powder
¾ teaspoon fenugreek seeds
40 g (1½ oz) roasted dried shrimp, ground
   using a mortar and pestle
80 ml (3 fl oz/⅓ cup) vegetable oil
1 large brown onion, chopped
3 garlic cloves, minced
2 slices of young ginger

1 sprig curry leaves, leaves picked
10 cm (4 inch) piece of lemongrass, cracked
   with the back of a knife
5 cm (2 inch) piece of pandan leaf (see glossary)
450 ml (16 fl oz) thick coconut milk

To make the meat curry, place all the meat in a large heavy-based saucepan and cover with the water. Place over high heat and bring to the boil, skimming the surface of any scum. Add the cardamom, cinnamon, cloves and salt and simmer for 15 minutes. Strain, reserving the stock to cook the rice.

Mix the remaining spices and ground dried shrimp into the meat and set aside.

Heat the oil in a large heavy-based saucepan over medium heat, add the onion, garlic, ginger, curry leaves, lemongrass and pandan leaf and cook for 4–5 minutes or until fragrant and the onion is soft and translucent. Add the meat mixture and cook, stirring constantly, for 5 minutes.

Add the coconut milk, bring to the boil and simmer for 8–12 minutes or until reduced by half and the curry is moist but not runny.

Meanwhile, to make steamed rice, follow the instructions on page 219 using the reserved meat stock instead of water to cook the rice.

Preheat the oven to 180°C (360°F/Gas 4).

To assemble the lump rice parcels, run the banana leaves over an open flame to soften. Arrange 2 leaves in a cross and place 1 cup of the steamed rice in the centre. Using a spoon, spread 25 ml (¾ fl oz) of the coconut cream over the rice. Arrange some of the meat curry, eggplant pickle, 3 meatballs and 5 banana chips around the rice. Fold the banana leaves over the filling to enclose and secure with toothpicks. Repeat with the remaining leaves and filling.

Place the parcels on a baking tray, making sure the opening is at the top. Bake for 12 minutes or until the banana leaves start to brown. Remove from the oven, place a parcel on each plate and let guests open them at the table. Serve with the tomato sambal and sambal terasi on the side.

Note *When cooking with whole leaves, such as pandan leaf, or spices, such as cinnamon sticks, make sure to remove them before serving.*

CHICKEN LAP LAP

THE 24-HOUR MARKET IN PORT VILLA, VANUATU, IS AN AMAZING PLACE. THE VARIETY AND DIVERSITY OF THE FOOD AVAILABLE IS ASTOUNDING – FROM ANY TYPE OF ROOT VEGETABLE TO HUGE PILES OF MANGOES AND ALL OF THE TROPICAL FRUITS IN SEASON. YOU DON'T HAVE TO GO FAR AROUND THE MARKET TO FIND LIVE COCONUT CRABS, LAND CRABS AND ALL SORTS OF LIVE SHELLFISH. THROUGHOUT THE MARKET AN AROMA GENTLY WAFTS ITS WAY TO YOUR NOSTRILS. IT EVENTUALLY GRABS YOU AND DRAWS YOU INTO THE CENTRE OF THE MARKET WHERE TWO ROWS OF COLOURFULLY-DRESSED LADIES SELL THIS LOCAL SPECIALITY. CHICKEN LAP LAP: STARCHY, FILLING, SLIGHTLY SMOKY AND INCREDIBLY TASTY. IT CAN BE MADE WITH ANY STARCHY VEGETABLE OR FRUIT, SUCH AS CASSAVA, BANANA, SWEET POTATO OR TARO, OR A COMBINATION OF ALL. MY FAVOURITE IS SWEET POTATO AND GREEN BANANA. YOU CAN ALSO MAKE THE FILLING USING PORK OR SEAFOOD INSTEAD OF CHICKEN.

SERVES 6

5 large banana leaves, centre spines removed
2 green (unripe) bananas, grated
3 large sweet potatoes (yams), grated
1 wombok (Chinese cabbage), leaves washed and roughly chopped
1 bunch English spinach, roots trimmed, leaves washed and roughly chopped
salt and ground black pepper
1 x 1.4 kg (3 lb) free-range chicken, butterflied
2 tablespoons vegetable oil
500 ml (17 fl oz/2 cups) coconut milk
1 onion, finely chopped
1 garlic clove, minced
½ bunch spring onions (scallions) (green parts only), sliced

Preheat the oven to 180°C (360°F/Gas 4).

Run the banana leaves over an open flame for 30 seconds to soften. Overlap the leaves on a large baking tray to make the base for a parcel.

Mix the grated bananas and sweet potato together in a bowl. Mix the chopped wombok and spinach together in a separate bowl. Season both mixtures with salt and pepper.

Season the chicken with salt and pepper.

Heat the oil in a large heavy-based frying pan over high heat. When the oil has just started to smoke, add the chicken, skin side down. Cook for 2–3 minutes, until golden. Turn the chicken over to brown the other side.

To assemble, place half of the wombok and spinach mixture into the centre of the banana leaves. Spread the mixture out enough to fit the chicken on top, but leaving enough of the banana leaf to fold around the filling to make a parcel. Top with the sweet potato and banana mixture and then the chicken, skin side up. Cover with the remaining wombok and spinach. Mix half of the coconut milk with the garlic and onion, then pour over the filling. Wrap the banana leaves around the chicken, making sure no filling can escape.

Bake in the preheated oven for 1 hour, or until the chicken is cooked through.

Remove from the oven, open the banana leaves and pour the remaining coconut milk on top. Garnish with the spring onion before serving.

VIGAN LONGGANISA

THIS IS THE BABY BROTHER OF THE CHORIZO. IT'S A BITE-SIZED SAUSAGE WITH A UNIQUE FILIPINO FLAVOUR. I WAS LUCKY ENOUGH TO BE INVITED INTO A SMALL FACTORY TO ASSIST IN THE MANUFACTURE OF THESE LITTLE SAUSAGES. THE RECIPE IS A TIGHTLY HELD SECRET, BUT WITH A BIT OF PRODDING I WAS GIVEN ENOUGH CLUES TO CREATE MY OWN VERSION. WHEN COOKING THESE SAUSAGES, PLACE THEM IN A POT WITH A LITTLE BIT OF WATER AND BOIL THEM. ONCE THE WATER HAS EVAPORATED, THE OIL FROM WITHIN THE SAUSAGE WILL BE ENOUGH TO COOK IT.

MAKES 50

800 g (1 lb 12 oz) boneless lean pork shoulder, coarsely ground
400 g (14 oz) pork fat, coarsely ground
1½ heads garlic, minced
60 g (2¼ oz/¼ cup firmly packed) soft brown sugar
2 teaspoons sweet paprika
1½ teaspoons salt
1 teaspoon coarsely cracked black pepper
1 teaspoon chilli flakes (optional)
⅓ teaspoon ground bay leaf or 1 bay leaf, finely chopped
80 ml (3 fl oz/⅓ cup) apple cider vinegar
60 ml (2 fl oz/3 tablespoons) annatto oil (see glossary)
60 ml (2 fl oz/3 tablespoons) sweet soy sauce
thin natural sausage casings, soaked in cold water for 1 hour
vegetable oil, for cooking (optional)

Place all of the ingredients, except the casings, in a large bowl and, using very clean hands, combine well. Cover and refrigerate for 1 hour.

Using a piping bag fitted with a 16 mm (⅝ inch) wide nozzle, fill the casings, being careful not to overfill or the sausages will burst upon cooking. Tie the ends of the filled casings with kitchen twine, then twist at 10 cm (4 inch) intervals to form a link of sausages.

Place the sausages in a sealed container in the crisper compartment of the refrigerator for 2–5 days (see note).

To cook, place the desired amount of sausages in a heavy-based frying pan and add 1 cm (¼ inch) of water to the pan. Simmer over medium heat for about 10 minutes or until the water evaporates. Prick the sausages with a fork, then allow to cook in their own fat for 3–5 minutes or until the skin caramelises and turns reddish brown, adding a little oil to the pan if necessary.

Vigan longganisa is great served with garlic rice, fried or scrambled eggs and sliced tomatoes with spicy vinegar on the side.

Note *Alternatively sausages can be hung over a brick oven for 3–5 days to cure.*

DEVILLED BEEF

THIS IS ONE OF MY DAD'S FAVOURITE DISHES AND ANOTHER SPECIALTY OF GALLE FACE HOTEL IN COLOMBO, SRI LANKA. I AM NOT SURE OF ITS ORIGINS BUT IT SEEMS TO BE A MIX BETWEEN A CHINESE SWEET AND SOUR DISH AND A EUROPEAN STEW. IT IS FOUND ON NEARLY EVERY MENU, BUT IF NOT, YOU CAN SIMPLY REQUEST IT AS EVERYONE KNOWS HOW TO MAKE IT. IT IS PERFECT WITH A COLD BEER.

SERVES 6

50 ml (1¾ fl oz) vegetable oil
1 onion, cut into 2 cm (¾ inch) pieces
1 leek (white part only), cut into 2 cm (¾ inch) pieces
1 sprig curry leaves, leaves picked
2 garlic cloves, thinly sliced
2 banana capsicum (peppers), cut into thin rings
300 g (10½ oz) beef fillet or sirloin, thinly sliced against the grain
2 long red chillies, thinly sliced
50 ml (1¾ fl oz) Sri Lankan chilli tomato sauce (ketchup) (see glossary)
2 vine-ripened tomatoes, cut into 8 wedges

Heat the oil in a heavy-based saucepan over high heat until just smoking, add the onion, leek, curry leaves and garlic and cook for 4 minutes or until the onion and leek are just soft but still have a crunch. Add the banana capsicum and cook for 3 minutes or until soft.

Add the beef and red chilli and cook for 3 minutes. Add the tomato sauce and tomato and cook for 3 minutes or until the meat is cooked.

Tanna chicken (see page 114).

TANNA CHICKEN

THIS DISH IS INSPIRED BY THE CHINESE BEGGAR'S CHICKEN, USING THE LOCAL INGREDIENTS I HAD TO HAND AT TANNA IN VANUATU — AND IT WORKED PERFECTLY. I LOVE IT WHEN YOU'RE IN THESE KINDS OF SITUATIONS, WITH FOREIGN INGREDIENTS AND PEOPLE, AND EXPERIENCE IS THE ONLY THING YOU HAVE TO WORK WITH. THAT'S WHEN SO MANY DOORS OPEN AND YOU LEARN THE MOST AMAZING THINGS AND CREATE SOME REALLY TASTY DISHES ALONG THE WAY.

SERVES 4 (PICTURED PAGE 113)

1 x 1.6 kg (3 lb 8 oz) free-range chicken
2 garlic cloves
2 cm (¾ inch) piece of ginger, grated
6 small red or green chillies
6 whole cloves
2 tablespoons sweet soy sauce
1 tablespoon chilli sauce
1 bunch English spinach, roots trimmed, leaves washed well and torn
juice of 1 lime
salt and ground black pepper, to taste
4–5 large banana leaves
olive oil, for greasing
cucumber salad (see page 170), to serve

SAND CASING

2 kg (4 lb 6 oz) sand
1 kg (2 lb 3 oz) fine salt
12 eggwhites

Preheat the oven to 250°C (500°F/Gas 9).

Trim the chicken and ensure that the skin covering the breasts remains intact.

Using a mortar and pestle, grind the garlic, ginger, chilli and cloves until a smooth paste forms. Rub the paste all over the chicken, inside and out.

Combine the sweet soy sauce and chilli sauce together and rub it all over the chicken.

Stuff the chicken with the spinach, then drizzle the lime over the skin and season well with salt and pepper.

To wrap the chicken, soften the banana leaves by running them over a flame for about 30 seconds or until they turn oily (see note). Place two banana leaves on a work surface in a cross pattern and lightly oil them.

Place the wrapped chicken, breast-side down, on the leaves and wrap it so both leaves cover the bird evenly. If necessary, use another leaf. Tie it well with kitchen twine and set aside.

To make the sand casing, mix all of the ingredients in a large bowl until you get a sloppy paste.

Place another two banana leaves on the work surface in a cross pattern and place half of the sand casing on it. Place the chicken, breast side up, onto the paste and put the rest of the paste on top. Ensure the entire parcel is coated evenly with the sand casing, then wrap it up the same way as the first wrapping and secure with kitchen twine. Place the parcel on a baking tray and bake for 1½ hours.

Remove from the oven and remove the outer banana leaves. It should be a hard rock. Leave for 5 minutes.

To serve, either take the chicken in its rock casing to the table and break it open with a hammer or crack it open in the kitchen and unwrap the chicken from its second covering of banana leaves. Serve the chicken with its cooking juices and the cucumber salad.

Note *Running banana leaves over an open flame helps to soften them, making them easier to handle.*

TWICE-COOKED SPICED DUCK

I COOKED THIS DISH ON THE ISLAND OF TERNATE IN EASTERN INDONESIA.

SERVES 4

1 Aylesbury duck (about 1.4 kg/3 lb), cleaned
2 teaspoons coarse salt
2 teaspoons coarsely ground black pepper
1 bunch English spinach, roughly chopped
5 bamboo skewers
6 whole cloves
1–2 large banana leaves
2 long red chillies, finely chopped
1 lime, quartered
2 French shallots, quartered

SPICE MIX

25 g (⅞ oz) turmeric, roughly chopped
1 cm (½ inch) piece of young ginger, roughly chopped
½ stick lemongrass (white part only), roughly chopped
2 candlenuts (see glossary)
3 garlic cloves
1 French shallot, roughly chopped
2 kaffir lime leaves, torn
2 long red chillies, roughly chopped
50 ml (1¾ fl oz) vegetable oil

To make the spice mix, using a spice grinder or mortar and pestle, blend all of the ingredients to a coarse paste.

Rub the duck inside and out with the salt and pepper, followed by the spice paste. Stuff the cavity with the spinach. Using the skewers, seal the stomach cavity, leaving the skewers sticking out of the duck.

Stud the skin of the duck evenly with the cloves.

Run the banana leaves over an open flame to soften them (see note), then wrap the duck completely in the leaves, using the protruding skewers to attach and secure the leaves.

Place the duck in a steamer basket, cover with the lid and steam over a saucepan of simmering water for 1½ hours.

Preheat the oven to 180°C (360°F/Gas 4).

Remove the duck from the steamer basket, place, breast-side up, in a large roasting tray and roast for 30 minutes or until the skin is brown and crisp.

Remove the duck from the oven and cut into 8 pieces.

Present on a banana leaf, garnished with the chilli, lime quarters and shallot quarters.

Note *Running banana leaves over an open flame helps to soften them, making them easier to handle.*

BEEF WITH SAUTÉED MUSHROOMS AND BITTER GOURD

I CAME UP WITH THIS DISH ON THE ISLAND OF SIQUIJOR IN THE PHILIPPINES. IT IS SAID THAT WHILE ON THIS ISLAND IF SOMEONE TOUCHES YOU ON THE SHOULDER, YOU SHOULD IMMEDIATELY DO IT BACK, OR ELSE THEY MAY TAKE ALL YOUR POWER.

SERVES 6

1.2 kg (2 lb 10 oz) trimmed beef sirloin, cut into 50 g (1¾ oz) pieces
salt and ground black pepper, to taste
3 litres (6 pt 6 fl oz) beef stock
100 g (3½ oz) butter
100 ml (3½ fl oz) olive oil
6 garlic cloves, minced with a large pinch of salt
150 g (5 oz) French shallots, finely diced
50 g (1¾ oz) fresh shiitake mushrooms, trimmed
40 g (1½ oz) wood ear mushrooms
2 tablespoon Mexican spices (see glossary)
100 ml (3½ fl oz) red wine
2 bitter gourds (see glossary), halved lengthways, seeds removed and finely diced
2 carrots, finely diced

GARNISH
200 ml (7 fl oz) vegetable oil
4 garlic cloves, thinly sliced
4 French shallots, thinly sliced
½ bitter gourd, seeds removed and thinly sliced

Preheat the oven to 140°C (285°F/Gas 1).

Trim the beef, then rub with salt and pepper. Place in a heavy-based casserole dish with the stock and bring to a gentle boil. Cover with a lid, transfer to the oven and cook for 3 hours or until very tender. Remove the beef with a slotted spoon and set aside.

Skim the cooking liquid and simmer over low heat until the stock has reduced by three-quarters. Remove from the heat and keep warm.

Meanwhile, to make the garnish, heat the oil in a frying pan to 160°C (320°F) or until a cube of bread browns in 30–35 seconds, and fry the garlic, shallot and gourd separately until golden and crisp. Remove with a slotted spoon, drain on paper towel and set aside.

Heat half of the butter and all of the oil in a heavy-based frying pan over medium–high heat. When the butter is frothy and just starts to turn brown, add the garlic and shallot and stir for a few seconds, then add the mushrooms and stir-fry for 3 minutes. Strain through a fine mesh sieve placed over a heatproof bowl. Set the mushroom mixture aside.

Return the strained liquid to the pan over medium–high heat. When hot, dust the beef in the Mexican spices, add to the pan and cook until golden all over.

Add the wine and simmer until reduced by half. Remove the beef with a slotted spoon and set aside.

Add 150 ml (5 fl oz) of the reduced stock to the pan and simmer until reduced by half. Add the gourd, carrot and remaining butter, reduce the heat to as low as possible and shake the pan so all the butter is incorporated into the sauce.

To serve, arrange the beef on a plate and top with the mushrooms and spoon over some of the cooking juices. Place a spoonful of the gourd and carrot sauce at the base of each piece of beef, then sprinkle a little pile of the fried onion, garlic and gourd chips about the plate. Serve immediately.

SPANISH-STYLE CHORIZO, CRISPY PORK BELLY AND GARLIC BREADCRUMBS

THIS IS A FILIPINO, SPANISH AND MEXICAN-INFLUENCED DISH FROM THE BEAUTIFUL TOWN OF VIGAN, IN THE PHILIPPINES. VIGAN IS VERY SPANISH, WITH VALENCIA ORANGES EVERYWHERE, AND IT IS THE IDEAL BACKDROP FOR SITTING ON THE STREET ENJOYING A DISH SUCH AS THIS ONE.

SERVES 6

500 g (1 lb 2 oz) crusty bread
125 ml (4 fl oz/½ cup) water
200 g (7 oz) boneless pork belly, skin on
5 fresh Spanish chorizo
250 ml (8½ fl oz/1 cup) water
125 ml (4 fl oz/½ cup) olive oil
6 garlic cloves, unpeeled
1 tablespoon smoked Spanish paprika
salt and ground black pepper, to taste
2 oranges, peeled and sliced into rings
chive flowers and flat-leaf (Italian) parsley leaves, to garnish

CHILLI VINEGAR
100 ml (3½ fl oz) cane vinegar (see glossary)
6 red bird's eye chillies, finely chopped
1 red Asian shallot, finely chopped
1 garlic clove, thinly sliced

Tear the bread into chunks and place in a sealable container. Add a pinch of salt and the water, seal with a lid, shake to combine, and refrigerate overnight.

Place the pork belly in a steamer basket, cover with a lid and steam over a wok of boiling water for 30 minutes.

Preheat the oven to 240°C (475°F/Gas 8) fan-forced.

Remove the pork from the steamer basket and while the pork is still hot, using a sharp knife, lightly score the skin at 1 cm (½ inch) intervals, then rub salt into the incisions.

Place the pork, skin side up, on a sheet of foil and fold in the sides up to the skin, leaving the skin uncovered. Place in a deep roasting tray and fill with water to reach halfway up the pork. Roast for 30 minutes or until the skin is crisp and crackled.

Remove from the oven and water bath, cut the crackling away from the meat and scrape off any remaining fat. Cut the crackling into strips and set aside. Cut the meat into 1 cm (½ inch) thick slices and keep warm until needed.

Place the chorizo and water in a heavy-based saucepan over high heat and cook until the water has evaporated and the sausages start to cook in their own oil. Reduce the heat to low and continue cooking until the chorizo are a nice golden colour. Remove from the pan with a slotted spoon, leaving the oil in the pan. Thickly slice and set aside.

Add the pork belly to the pan and cook over high heat for 2 minutes or until hot. Remove from the pan and set aside.

Add the oil and garlic cloves to the pan and cook over medium heat until the cloves are soft inside and the skin is golden. Remove with a slotted spoon leaving the oil in the pan and set aside.

Squeeze the bread between your hands to remove excess water, add to the pan and cook over medium–high heat until golden and crunchy. Add the paprika, return the pork, chorizo and garlic to the pan and stir until heated through.

To make the chilli vinegar, combine all of the ingredients in a small bowl and set aside.

Serve the pork mixture with the orange slices and crackling, scatter over the chive flowers and parsley and serve with the chilli vinegar on the side.

FILIPINO-STYLE SUCKLING PIG LECHON BABOY

SPIT-ROASTED SUCKLING PIG IS ALWAYS A CROWD FAVOURITE AT A PARTY, BUT IT IS HARD TO PERFECT. A SPIT-ROASTER CAN BE EASILY OBTAINED FROM A BARBECUE-HIRE SERVICE, AVAILABLE IN MOST AREAS. THEY CAN SUPPLY YOU WITH ALL THE UTENSILS YOU'LL NEED, AS WELL AS THE COALS. MOST BUTCHERS WILL HAPPILY ARRANGE A SUCKLING PIG BUT IT'S BEST TO GIVE THEM NOTICE. ALWAYS INSIST ON A FRESH YOUNG PIG. I RECOMMEND STUFFING THE PIG WITH ONIONS, APPLES, CARROTS, GARLIC AND PARSLEY BUT THE FILIPINOS FILL THE CAVITY ONLY WITH LEMONGRASS.

SERVES 12 GENEROUSLY

1 x 8 kg (17 lb 10 oz) suckling pig
10 garlic cloves, crushed
coarse salt and ground black pepper
roughly chopped vegetables (such as onion, carrot,
    apples garlic and parsley), to fill the cavity
750 ml (25 fl oz/3 cups) salt-reduced soy sauce
750 ml (25 fl oz/3 cups) olive oil

EQUIPMENT
barbecue coals
1 spit-roaster
heavy wire, to stitch the belly of the pig
    (this is usually provided with the spit)
1 pair of pliers
a metal shovel, for moving the hot coals about

First, light the barbecue coals. The coals are not ready to use until they have turned white (no flame should be present when cooking). This will take 1–2 hours.

With a sharp knife, remove the tail and ears of the pig. Turn the pig over and remove the kidneys and any loose fat.

Rub the surface of the pig with some of the garlic, massaging well. This will add flavour as well as moistening the skin. Once thoroughly rubbed in, place the remaining garlic inside the cavity of the pig.

Apply a liberal amount of salt to the skin and massage well. The salt is crucial to dry the skin and create perfect crackling. Apply a liberal amount of pepper to the skin. Liberally season the cavity too.

To ensure an even roast, completely fill the cavity with the vegetables, then stitch the cavity with the heavy wire to seal tightly.

Massage the soy sauce into the skin. This will help create a golden brown colour.

To mount the pig on the spit, place, belly down, on a work surface or table and insert the spit-mounting from the rear of the pig. Ensure you have read the instructions that come with your spit. It is vital that the pig does not spin in the rotisserie — check it prior to loading onto the spit.

Using the shovel, move the bulk of the coals to the edges, underneath the legs and shoulders, with only a small amount of coals under the mid-section. The legs and shoulders are the thickest areas and require the most heat. As the pig cooks, ensure the colour remains even. If any patches are lighter in colour, move more coals under that area. If an area is darkening too quickly, move the coals away. Occasionally baste with oil to improve the crackling. In the late stages of roasting, the vegetables in the cavity of the pig will soften and release their juices. It's a good idea to wipe the juices away to maintain an even finish on the skin.

When the knuckles of the pig start to become exposed, it's a sign that the pig is nearly done. It's a good idea to stop the rotisserie motor and insert a small knife into the thickest part of the pig — the leg is ideal. Leave the knife in for 30 seconds, then remove it and check that the tip of the knife is hot. Alternatively, insert a meat thermometer into the leg and if it registers 70°C (158°F), it is done. An 8 kg pig will require about 1½–2 hours roasting time.

When the pig is done, it's important to move it to the place you wish to serve it prior to removing the spit-mounting from it, as there will be little connective tissue holding it together and the pig may fall apart if it's moved after the bar is removed. Turn the rotisserie off and then use tea towels or oven mitts to handle the spit-mounting. You will need two people to move the pig. Once the pig is in its final position, carefully remove the spit-mounting, carve and serve.

Seafood

AUNTY TAPUNA'S CRAB AND GREEN MANGO

PERCHED HIGH ABOVE THE OCEAN IN THE COOK ISLANDS, AUNTY TAPUNA HAS HER OWN LITTLE MARKET GARDEN IN HER YARD AND A GOOD RELATIONSHIP WITH ALL THE FISHER PEOPLE OF THE ISLAND. BELOW HER HOUSE IS A LOVELY LITTLE RESTAURANT WHERE SHE SERVES ONLY THE FRESHEST FOOD. HER CRABS ARE FAMOUS ALL OVER THE ISLANDS. SHE GENEROUSLY SHARED HER FAMOUS CRAB RECIPE WITH ME, AND THE BEST PART WAS HUNTING THE CRABS THE NIGHT BEFORE WITH DAVE THE FISHERMAN.

SERVES 2

1 live mud crab (about 1.2 kg / 2 lb 10 oz)
100 ml (3 ½ fl oz) olive oil
1 onion, finely chopped
1 teaspoon chopped garlic
1¼ teaspoons finely chopped ginger
2 tablespoon chopped mixed herbs (such as coriander/cilantro, basil, parsley, chives, dill, spring onion/scallion)
50 g (1 ¾ oz) butter
salt and ground black pepper, to taste
4 green mangoes (they must be yellow inside), peeled and roughly chopped
1 long red chilli, sliced
100 ml (3 ½ fl oz) white wine

Put the crabs in the freezer for 1 hour to immobilise them or in a bucket of iced water for 15 minutes. Pull off the top shell, pull out the spongy grey gills and remove the guts. Chop the crab into 6 pieces and crack the large claws but leave them attached.

Heat the oil in a large heavy-based saucepan over medium heat. When hot, add the onion, garlic and ginger and cook for 5–6 minutes or until soft. Add the herbs and cook for 30 seconds or until fragrant. Add the butter, season with salt and pepper, then add the chilli and half the mango and stir for 3 minutes or until the mango starts to break down.

Add the wine to slow the cooking process, then add the crab, placing the claws in the pan first. Add the remaining mango on top, cover with foil, then a lid and cook over high heat, shaking the pan often to avoid sticking, for 5–7 minutes or until steam pushes through the lid. Carefully remove the lid and serve immediately.

RAW TREVALLY SALAD WITH POMEGRANATE

WHEN I WAS IN AITUTAKI IN THE COOK ISLANDS FILMING *ISLAND FEAST*, I WENT SPEARFISHING WITH ONE OF THE LOCALS, DAVE. HE GUIDED ME OUT ONTO THE REEF, HE HAD NO SHOES ON, THE TIDE WAS RISING AND THERE WAS A HUGE SWELL. WE VENTURED TO THE EDGE OF THE REEF AND WERE REWARDED WITH A BEAUTIFUL TREVALLY FOR DINNER. I CREATED THIS DISH WHEN WE GOT BACK ON LAND.

SERVES 6

500 g (1 lb 2 oz) sashimi-grade trevally (see note), trimmed
1 ripe but firm papaya, preferably red, peeled, seeds removed, quartered and cut into thin 2 x 3 cm (¾ x 1¼ inch) diamonds
1 small pomegranate, seeds removed
1 telegraph (long) cucumber, peeled, shaved into ribbons using a vegetable peeler, core discarded
2 oranges, peeled, pith removed and segmented
3 spring onions (scallions), cut into julienne and placed in iced water, then drained
3 French shallots, thinly sliced
2 long red chillies, seeds removed and cut into julienne
spring onion and lime dressing (see page 194)

Cut the fish into 5 x 15 cm (2 x 6 inch) blocks, then thinly slice against the grain. Arrange the fish on plates, scatter over the remaining salad ingredients, drizzle over the dressing and serve immediately.

Note *Generally when using raw or barely cooked fish in a recipe, make sure it is sashimi grade. A good fishmonger will be able to give you this information.*

OCTOPUS, SURF CLAMS AND UDON NOODLE SALAD

THIS DISH IS INSPIRED BY KURA, A BEAUTIFUL OCTOPUS FISHERWOMAN FROM THE COOK ISLANDS WHO CATCHES OCTOPUS FOR HER GRANDMOTHER TO COOK. SHE TOLD ME OF A DAY WHEN ONE OCTOPUS WAS MUCH LARGER THAN NORMAL, SO WHEN SHE SPEARED IT, IT DRAGGED HER UNDER THE WATER AND GAVE HER A REAL FIGHT. SHE WON IN THE END THOUGH. AFTER CHATTING FOR A WHILE WITH HER, WE REALISED WE BOTH WENT TO THE SAME SCHOOL IN SYDNEY.

SERVES 6

24 surf clams or similar
salt, to taste
1 whole octopus, head cleaned (about 1.5 kg/3 lb 5 oz)
300 ml (10 fl oz) water, plus 200 ml extra (as necessary)
100 ml (3½ fl oz) olive oil
1 onion, finely chopped
2 cm (¾ inch) piece of ginger, finely chopped
¼ bunch flat-leaf (Italian) parsley, leaves picked
200 ml (7 fl oz) white wine
½ bunch garlic chives, finely chopped
juice of 2 limes
150 g (5 oz) organic udon noodles, cooked
2 tablespoons toasted sesame seeds
sesame and golden syrup dressing (see page 192)

Soak the clams in plenty of cold water combined with enough salt so it tastes like seawater. Leave to soak for 3–6 hours.

Place the whole octopus in a heavy-based saucepan with the 300 ml (10 fl oz) of water over low heat and cook until the moisture starts coming out, then cover with a lid, increase the heat to medium and cook for about 1 hour or until a knife goes through the thickest part of the tentacles without too much difficulty — you want the tentacles to have a bit of bite, not to be too soft. Check occasionally and if the liquid has evaporated, add the extra 200 ml (7 fl oz) of water and reduce the heat. Remove the tentacles and slice them on an angle into thin slices. Remove the tentacles and slice them on an angle into thin slices. (Reserve the head for another meal if desired.) Set aside.

Meanwhile, heat the oil in a heavy-based saucepan over high heat. When the oil starts to smoke, toss in the onion, ginger, parsley and clams and cook until the onion is fragrant. Add the wine, cover and cook for 2 minutes. Remove the lid and as each clam starts to open, remove it from the pan, as this is an indicator that it is cooked.

Remove and discard half of each clam shell, leaving the flesh in the remaining half shell. Discard the cooking liquid.

Make each salad individually. Place some of the clams, octopus and garlic chives in a bowl and add 2 tablespoons of the dressing per serve, season to taste with some of the lime juice and mix well. Add 1 small handful of the noodles and combine. Garnish with some of the sesame seeds.

SEAFOOD CAKES WITH GRILLED BANANA AND ROASTED BREADFRUIT

I THINK I MIGHT BE THE FIRST PERSON TO COOK ON THE EDGE OF THE MIGHTY VOLCANO IN TANNA, VANUATU. I COOKED THIS DISH FOR THE TELEVISION SHOW BUT I ALSO COOKED A LUNCH OF STEAMED YAMS AND HARD-BOILED EGGS FOR THE CREW IN ONE OF THE FISSURES OF THE VOLCANO. AFTER ALL THE FILMING WAS DONE, WE WENT TO THE VILLAGE WHERE MY GUIDES CAME FROM AND THEY SHOWED ME WHERE THE HOT SPRING FROM THE VOLCANO MET THE OCEAN. IT WAS STUNNING. THE HOT WATER MIXED WITH THE COOL OCEAN WATER AND ALL THE KIDS WERE SWIMMING IN IT. ONE OF THE BOYS ASKED ME IF I SURFED, AND WHEN I SAID YES, HE TOOK ME INTO THE JUNGLE AND WITH A LARGE BUSH KNIFE HE RIPPED THE BARK OFF A MASSIVE TREE. WE WENT BACK TO THE BEACH AND USED THE PIECE OF BARK AS A SURFBOARD!

SERVES 6

6 large banana leaves
olive oil, for brushing
200 g (7 oz) raw lobster or prawn (shrimp) meat
400 g (14 oz) white fish fillets, skinned and pin-boned
2 garlic cloves, finely chopped
2 cm (¾ inch) piece of ginger, finely chopped
2 red Asian shallots, finely chopped
2 small green chillies, finely chopped
1 egg
roasted breadfruit (see page 218) and grilled banana
    (see page 218), to serve

CARROT SALAD

1 large carrot, coarsely grated
1 small green papaya, peeled and finely grated
1 small red chilli, finely chopped, plus extra to serve
juice of 1 lime, plus extra to serve
salt and ground black pepper, to taste

Preheat the oven to 230°C (450°F/Gas 8) and place a pizza stone or heavy-based baking tray inside to preheat.

Cut the banana leaves into twelve 30 cm (12 inch) squares and run over an open flame for 30 seconds to soften. Lightly brush the leaves with oil. Set aside.

Cut the seafood into small cubes with a knife — do not use a food processor as this will make the mixture rubbery. Combine the seafood with the garlic, ginger, shallot and chilli in a large bowl and mix together well. Add the egg and mix until well combined. Set aside to rest for 5 minutes.

To make the carrot salad, place all of the ingredients in a bowl, season with salt and pepper and mix well.

To assemble, layer two banana leaves on top of each other and form 100 g (3½ oz) of the seafood mixture in the centre in a log. Wrap like a parcel, making sure no mixture can escape and secure with kitchen twine. Repeat with the remaining banana leaves and seafood mixture. Place the parcels on the pizza stone or tray and bake for 5 minutes, then turn and bake for another 5 minutes.

To serve, unwrap the parcels, reserving any juices. Pour the juices over the seafood cakes and serve with the carrot salad, roasted breadfruit, grilled banana, lime and chillies.

PRAWNS WITH OKRA SAMBAL

SERVES 6

2 potatoes
2 carrots
1 large beetroot (beet)
12 prawns (shrimp), shelled and deveined
pinch of ground black pepper
½ teaspoon salt
1 tablespoon butter
juice of 1 lime

PANGRATTATO

50 ml (1¾ fl oz) olive oil
50 g (1¾ oz) butter
2 garlic cloves, very finely chopped
2 thick slices bread, crusts removed and
  cut into small cubes
1 prawn (shrimp), shelled and deveined, chopped
salt and ground black pepper, to taste

OKRA SAMBAL

1 litre (34 fl oz/4 cups) vegetable oil
300 g (10½ oz) okra, trimmed and halved lengthways
½ teaspoon salt
pinch of black pepper
juice of 1 lime

GARNISHES

1 large tomato, finely diced
1 long red chilli, thinly sliced
Maldive fish flakes (see glossary), for sprinkling
½ red onion, finely diced
6 gotu kola leaves (see glossary)
lime halves

Peel the potatoes, carrots and beetroot and scoop into balls using a small melon baller. Keep the beetroot balls separate but you can combine the potato and carrot.

Place the potato and carrot in a large saucepan of water and the beetroot in a separate pan of water, bring to the boil over medium heat and cook for 10–15 minutes or until just cooked. Drain and refresh in iced water to stop them cooking further. Drain again and set aside.

To make the pangrattato, heat the oil and butter in a large saucepan over high heat until the mixture starts to froth, add the garlic and cook until fragrant. Add the bread and cook, stirring occasionally, until crisp and golden.

Add the prawn and cook, stirring to combine, until cooked through. Season with salt and pepper. Remove from the heat and drain in a fine mesh sieve placed over a heatproof bowl. Reserve the cooking oil. Chop the bread mixture into smaller cubes and set aside until ready to serve.

To make the okra sambal, heat the oil in a large deep-sided saucepan to 180°C (360°F) or until a cube of bread turns golden in 15 seconds. Add the okra, in batches, and deep-fry for a few minutes or until golden. Remove with a slotted spoon and drain on paper towel. Place in a bowl with the salt, pepper and lime juice and toss to coat. Set aside.

To cook the prawns, trim the prawns if necessary, so they are a similar size to ensure even cooking, and season with pepper. Heat the reserved oil from the pangrattato in a medium frying pan over medium heat, season with salt, and when the oil is hot, add the prawns and cook for a few minutes on one side, then turn the prawns over and cook the other side for 1 minute or until cooked through. Remove the prawns from the pan, leaving the oil in the pan, and set aside.

Add the potato, carrot and beetroot to the same pan and cook over low heat, stirring to coat the vegetables in the leftover oil, until warmed through. Season if necessary, stir in the butter and lime juice, then remove from the heat.

To serve, place the okra sambal on platter, top with the prawns and scatter over the vegetable balls and pangrattato. Scatter the garnishes over the entire dish to finish.

COCONUT CRAB AND SEAFOOD PLATTER

THE FLAVOUR OF THE COCONUT CRAB IS DELICIOUS. HUNTING THEM IN VANUATU WAS DANGEROUS BUT I WAS FORTUNATE ENOUGH TO HAVE THE VILLAGE CHIEF MOR MOR AS MY GUIDE. HE IS A WISE MAN WITH A SUSTAINABLE OUTLOOK. HE TOOK ONLY WHAT HE NEEDED AS HE WANTED TO PRESERVE THE BOUNTIES OF THE OCEAN FOR HIS CHILDREN AND GRANDCHILDREN.

SERVES 6

1 coconut crab or mud crab (about 1.5 kg/3 lb 5 oz), cleaned
1 litre (34 fl oz/4 cups) second-extract coconut milk (see note)
6 small green chillies, coarsely chopped
juice of 2 limes
salt, to taste
2 parrotfish or other reef fish (about 2 kg/4 lb 6 oz each), scaled and cleaned
10 small land crabs (about 100 g/3½ oz each) or blue swimmer crabs
2 kg (4 lb 6 oz) large sea snails
boiled cassava (see glossary), to serve
chilli, lime and seawater sauce (see page 194)

Place the coconut crab, coconut milk, chilli, lime juice and a pinch of salt in a large saucepan over high heat and bring to the boil, then cover and cook for 9 minutes. Using tongs and a slotted spoon, remove the crab and set aside.

Add the fish to the pan, reduce the heat to medium and simmer for 12 minutes or until just cooked through. Remove from the pan and set aside. Reserve some of the coconut sauce for serving.

Bring a large saucepan of salted water to the boil over high heat, add the land crabs, bring back to the boil and cook for 6 minutes. Drain and set aside.

Preheat a barbecue grill to high. Cook the sea snails for 4 minutes (ideally you would cook these on a wire rack over an open fire).

To serve, break the coconut crab into pieces and crack the claws, then do the same with the smaller land crabs. Serve the crab, fish and sea snails on a large platter with the boiled cassava. Serve with the chilli, lime and seawater sauce and the reserved coconut sauce for dipping the seafood and cassava into.

Note *To make second-extract coconut milk, crack a coconut with the back of a large cleaver. Reserve the coconut water as it drains out. For this recipe you'll need 1 litre (34 fl oz/ 4 cups) of coconut water; if you don't have enough, top up with filtered water. Scrape out the white flesh and trim off the brown membrane. Grate the flesh with a hand-grater or in a food processor. Place the grated flesh and 250 ml (8½ fl oz/1 cup) filtered water in a blender and, using the pulse action, process until everything is well combined and the flesh is soft. Line a sieve with muslin (cheesecloth) and place over a bowl. Pour in the blended coconut, then gather the sides of the muslin and squeeze to extract as much liquid as possible from the flesh. This is known as first-extract coconut milk or coconut cream. Reserve this for another recipe. To make the second extract, repeat the process using the same coconut flesh and the reserved coconut water.*

GRILLED YELLOWTAIL WITH CASSAVA RICE AND STAR FRUIT SALAD

THE SEA GYPSIES OF INDONESIA ORIGINATED FROM MALAYSIA AND NOW LIVE IN THE BANDA SEA ON TINY ISLANDS OR ROCK ATOLLS. THEIR HOUSES ARE BUILT ON STILTS ABOVE THE OCEAN. WE WERE INVITED INTO SUCH A HOUSE, WHERE THIS SIMPLE BUT DELICIOUS MEAL WAS SLOW-COOKED OVER AN OPEN FIRE. THERE WAS LOTS OF SMOKE AND IT WAS UNBELIEVABLY HOT IN THE HOUSE, BUT EVERYONE WAS SO HAPPY TO HAVE US THERE. IT WAS CERTAINLY AN EXPERIENCE THAT I WILL REMEMBER FOR THE REST OF MY LIFE.

SERVES 6

12 whole yellowtail or slimy mackerel, scaled and cleaned
vegetable oil, for brushing
cassava rice (see page 216), to serve
star fruit salad (see page 167), to serve

Preheat a barbecue grill to medium-high. Lightly brush with oil and cook the fish for 4 minutes each side or until just cooked through.

Serve with the cassava rice and star fruit salad.

Note *To get a smoky flavour into the fish, you could rub a bit of liquid smoke on the fish or cook it over a wood fire.*

PERFECT GRILLED SALMON

SALMON IS ONE OF THE MOST POPULAR SPECIES OF FISH IN THE WORLD AT THE MOMENT, AND THERE ARE SO MANY DIFFERENT OPINIONS ABOUT THE BEST METHOD OF GRILLING THEM. FOLLOW THE INSTRUCTIONS BELOW AND YOU WON'T BE DISAPPOINTED.

coarse salt, for sprinkling
olive oil, for brushing
1 x 180 g (6½ oz) salmon fillet (per person), skinned
    and pin-boned
lemon wedges, to serve

Preheat a barbecue grill plate to high and sprinkle with salt. This will increase the heat conductivity. Apply a drizzle of oil over the salt.

Once the oil begins to smoke a little, it's ready. Reduce the heat to medium.

Place the salmon, presentation side down (the side which will face up on the plate when served), on the grill — be sure to lay the fillet down away from your body to avoid any hot oil splashing toward you.

As the salmon begins to cook, a white line of cooked flesh will creep up the side of the fillet. For a perfect medium–rare result, turn the fish when the white line has risen about one-third of the way up through the fillet. Continue grilling until the white line on the other side has risen about one-third of the way up the fillet.

If you are concerned about overcooking the thinner part of the fillet, position the fillet on the edge of the barbecue with the thin portion of the fish hanging over the edge — this will stop the thin portion from overcooking while allowing the thicker portion to continue to cook. Remove and serve immediately with lemon wedges alongside.

CHARRED BONITO WITH ACHARA

When we go to the markets we always look for the 'glamorous' fish, but take a bit of time and start to experiment with the less well-known fish. In most cases they are probably more sustainable. Take bonito, for example, which lays 100 million eggs at a time. Bonito is an underrated fish outside of the islands and if treated properly is a good substitute for tuna. When fresh it has a wonderful flavour, and slightly charring the skin adds a lovely smoky flavour to it.

SERVES 6

200 g (7 oz) piece of sashimi-grade bonito (see note), skin on, cut into 4 equal pieces
100 g (3½ oz) sea grapes (see glossary), picked, or wakame seaweed
1 small tomato, diced
2 small red onions, finely diced
soy sauce, to serve
achara (see page 183), to serve

VINAIGRETTE
juice of 10 calamansi lemons (see glossary) or regular lemons, strained
80 ml (3 fl oz/⅓ cup) rice wine
60 ml (2 fl oz/3 tablespoons) olive oil
2 tablespoons white sugar
salt and black pepper, to taste

Place the fish, skin side up, on a baking tray and place a lightly oiled wire rack on top of the fish. Using a kitchen blowtorch, sear the skin for 10 seconds or until the skin is just marked. Remove the rack and refrigerate the fish until needed.

Combine the sea grapes, tomato and onion in a bowl and set aside.

To make the vinaigrette, place all of the ingredients in a bowl, season with salt and pepper and combine well.

To serve, thinly slice the fish and arrange on plates. Sprinkle the sea grape salad over the top and serve the achara and soy sauce on the side. Finish the dish with a drizzle of the vinaigrette.

Note *Generally when using raw or barely cooked fish in a recipe, make sure it is sashimi grade. A good fishmonger will be able to give you this information.*

PAN-ROASTED PAINTED CRAYFISH AND FRIED ANCHOVIES

IF YOU CAN'T FIND PAINTED CRAYFISH, THE TASMANIAN ONES ARE A GREAT SUBSTITUTE BUT YOU CAN USE ANY CRAYFISH OR LOBSTERS IN THIS DISH. I COOKED THIS FOR THE MASTER BOATBUILDERS OF BIRA IN SOUTH-EAST SULAWESI, INDONESIA. THE BOATS, CALLED PHINISI, HAVE BEEN HAND-BUILT OUT OF TEAK FOR CENTURIES. THEY ARE AN AWE-INSPIRING THING TO SEE. WHEN I FIRST SAW THESE HUGE BOATS IN THE BOAT YARD I THOUGHT TO MYSELF THAT THIS COULD HAVE BEEN WHERE THE STORY OF NOAH'S ARK CAME FROM. THE BUGIS SAILORS FROM THESE PARTS SET SAIL INTO THE WIND, THEIR HOLDS FULL OF CLOVES AND NUTMEG DESTINED FOR EUROPE, WHERE THE SPICES WERE MORE VALUABLE THAN GOLD.

SERVES 4

2 live painted (tropical) crayfish (about 1 kg/2 lb 3 oz each)
100 ml (3½ fl oz) vegetable oil
250 ml (8½ fl oz/1 cup) water
cucumber sambal (see page 176), to serve

CHILLI AND LIME SALT
6 red and green bird's eye chillies
1 tablespoon sea salt
squeeze of lime juice

FRIED ANCHOVIES
5 cm (2 inch) piece of turmeric, sliced
4 small green chillies, sliced
5 cm (2 inch) piece of ginger, grated
3 spring onions (scallions) (white part only), thinly sliced
1 teaspoon salt
60 ml (2 fl oz/3 tablespoons) vegetable oil
200 g (7 oz) fresh anchovies, scaled and cleaned
750 ml (25 fl oz/3 cups) grapeseed or canola oil

To make the fried anchovies, combine the turmeric, chilli, ginger, spring onion, salt and vegetable oil in a shallow dish and mix well. Add the anchovies, turn to coat and leave for 30 minutes. When ready to serve, heat the grapeseed oil in a small wok over medium heat and fry the anchovies for 4 minutes or until golden and crisp. Remove with a slotted spoon and drain on paper towel. Set aside.

To kill the crayfish, place them in a large bucket of iced water and leave for 15 minutes, then drain. Halve lengthways using a cleaver or large knife. Clean out the heads, but do not wash in cold water. Alternatively, ask your fishmonger to do this for you, but only if you live close by and have an ice box to transport the lobsters home and plan to cook them immediately.

To make the chilli and lime salt, using a mortar and pestle, grind the chilli and salt together until a paste, then stir in the lime juice.

When you're ready to cook the crayfish, rub some of the chilli and lime salt all over the flesh. Heat the oil in a large heavy-based frying pan over high heat, add the crayfish and cook for 4 minutes or until light golden, but not crisp. Turn the crayfish over, add the water, cover and cook over medium heat for 5 minutes or until just cooked.

To serve, place the crayfish in the centre of a serving platter and arrange the fried anchovies alongside. Serve with the cucumber sambal and any remaining chilli and lime salt.

GRILLED BANANA PRAWNS WITH BLACK PEPPER AND CURRY LEAF SAUCE

I HAVE TO LAUGH ABOUT THIS DISH AS IT WAS THE FIRST ONE SHOWN ON MY FIRST SERIES, *MY SRI LANKA*. PEOPLE COMMENTED THAT THIS WAS NOT A SRI LANKAN DISH. WELL I HAVE TO AGREE, BUT THE IDEA THAT SOY, SESAME OR OYSTER SAUCE IS NOT USED IN SRI LANKAN COOKERY IS INCORRECT — THE SMALL CHINESE POPULATION OF SRI LANKA HAVE BEEN THERE FOR CENTURIES, AND SRI LANKANS REGARD CHOP SUEY AND CHOW MEIN AS PART OF THE SRI LANKAN DIET. ADD A BIT OF CREATIVE LICENCE AND WE HAVE THIS SAUCE. THE SAUCE HAS BEEN A TIGHTLY KEPT SECRET FOR MANY YEARS SO ENJOY IT AND PUT IT ON ANYTHING.

SERVES 6 AS A STARTER

2–3 pomelo or 6 ruby grapefruit segments
100 ml (3½ fl oz) vegetable oil, plus extra for shallow-frying
1 red onion, thinly sliced
½ cup freshly grated coconut
12 banana prawns (shrimp), shelled and deveined with tails intact
ground black pepper, to taste
black pepper and curry leaf sauce (see page 186), to serve
2 long red chillies, seeds removed and cut into julienne
2 sprigs curry leaves, leaves picked

Take each pomelo segment and separate the flesh to get short strands of 'pearls'. Set aside.

Heat 100 ml (3½ fl oz) of the oil in a frying pan over medium heat. Once hot, add the onion and cook until golden and crisp. Remove from the heat and leave to cool.

Mix the coconut and the onion together and set aside.

Season the prawns with pepper. Heat 2 cm (¾ inch) of oil in a wok over high heat. Once the oil reaches smoking point, add the prawns, one by one, and fry until crisp and just cooked, making sure the oil remains hot enough to avoid 'boiling' the prawns in the oil. Remove the prawns with a slotted spoon and place into a bowl.

To serve, intertwine pairs of the prawns and place each onto a plate. Spoon a small portion of the black pepper and curry leaf sauce on top of each pair of prawns. Top the prawns with a small portion of the onion mixture, some chilli, a few strands of the pomelo and some curry leaves.

SEARED WAHOO, SNAKE BEANS AND PAPAYA SALAD

I CAUGHT THIS BEAUTY OF A FISH IN THE COOK ISLANDS AND WAS INSPIRED BY THE LOCAL INGREDIENTS TO CREATE THIS DISH. IT WOULD SIT NICELY ON ANY TABLE AND WOULD BE A GREAT HIT AT A BARBECUE.

SERVES 6

1 bunch snake (yard-long) beans (about 150 g/5 oz), cut into 5 cm (2 inch) lengths
6 wahoo steaks (about 200 g/7 oz each)
1 tablespoon smoked sea salt
200 ml (7 fl oz) olive oil
100 g (3½ oz) butter, chopped
juice of 1 lime
baby mustard cress, to serve
red onion soubise (see page 183), to serve
papaya salad (see page 167), to serve

Bring a saucepan of salted water to the boil, add the snake beans, bring back to the boil, then drain and refresh in iced water. Drain again and set aside.

Season the fish with a little of the salt. Heat the oil in a large heavy-based frying pan over high heat and sprinkle over the remaining salt. Once the oil is hot, gently place the fish in the pan and cook for 4 minutes each side or until just cooked through. You may need to turn the heat down a little if the oil gets too hot. Remove from the pan and drain on paper towel. Set aside and keep warm.

Drain the oil from the pan, then add the butter and return to medium heat. Add the snake beans, lime juice and a little water and shake the pan until the sauce emulsifies and coats the beans. Remove from the heat.

To serve, place a little red onion soubise on each plate, then place a line of drained snake beans on top. Drape the fish over the beans and top with the papaya salad. Garnish with the baby mustard cress and serve immediately.

CRISPY DRIED FISH WITH RICE AND SAMBAL TERASI

I LOVE THE FLAVOUR OF DRIED FISH, AND WHEN PAIRED WITH THIS SPICY AND BOLD SAMBAL, IT IS ONE OF MY FAVOURITE DISHES, BUT THE INTENSE FLAVOURS ARE NOT FOR EVERYONE. SOAKING THE DRIED FISH IN BOILING WATER WILL TAKE AWAY A LOT OF ITS STRONG FLAVOUR. MY DAD CALLS DISHES LIKE THIS 'RICE-PULLERS' MEANING YOU JUST KEEP EATING MORE RICE WITH IT BECAUSE IT TASTES SO GOOD.

SERVES 4

2 dried groper or barramundi (about 400 g/14 oz each)
1 litre (34 fl oz/4 cups) vegetable oil
sambal terasi (see page 180), to serve
lime wedges, chopped chilli and steamed rice
   (see page 219), to serve

To reconstitute the dried fish, place it in a heatproof bowl and cover with boiling water. Leave until cool, then drain, rinse and pat dry.

Heat the oil in a large saucepan or wok to 190°C (375°F) or until a cube of bread turns golden in 10 seconds. Deep-fry the fish, in batches, if necessary, until golden and crisp. Remove with a slotted spoon and drain on paper towel.

Serve with the sambal terasi, lime wedges, chilli and a bowl of rice.

WHOLE FISH UMU AT HOME

AN UMU (ALSO KNOWN AS A LOVO OR HĀNGI) IS A POPULAR TRADITIONAL WAY OF COOKING THROUGHOUT THE PACIFIC ISLANDS. THIS RECIPE WILL HELP YOU ACHIEVE THE SIGNATURE TASTE OF UMU-COOKED FISH IN YOUR HOME KITCHEN WITHOUT THE NEED TO DIG UP THE BACKYARD! BUT DO NOT ATTEMPT THIS IN A GAS OVEN.

SERVES 6

1 large hessian sack (see note)
salt and ground black pepper, to taste
1 x 4 kg (8 lb 13 oz) fish (such as groper, snapper or coral trout)
¼ bunch dill, chopped
¼ bunch flat-leaf (Italian) parsley, leaves chopped
6 large banana leaves (you will need enough to wrap the fish in 2 layers)
200 ml (7 fl oz) smoky barbecue sauce
1 fresh coconut, flesh grated, to serve
coconut cream sauce (see page 182), to serve
lime halves, to serve

Soak the hessian sack in water for 2 hours. You need to make sure it is well soaked as you don't want it to catch fire in the oven.

Preheat the oven (must not be gas) to 220°C (430°F).

Rub salt and pepper all over the fish. Massage in the herbs, then splash the barbecue sauce all over the fish.

Lay the fish in a double layer of banana leaves and wrap it, making sure it is completely sealed. Place the parcel, fold side down, in a large roasting tray. Cover with the hessian sack and roast for about 1½ hours. If the hessian sack is drying out, pour over some water to ensure it is moist at all times. To check whether the fish is cooked, press it lightly just below the head and if it gives, the fish is done.

Once cooked, remove the fish from the oven, carefully lift it out of the tray, place on a large serving platter and unwrap the banana leaves.

Cover the fish with the grated coconut and serve with the coconut cream sauce and lime halves.

Note *Ask your local coffee roaster for a hessian sack.*

CRISP HERRINGS WITH A SPICY SRI LANKAN SALAD

THALPE, IN SOUTHERN SRI LANKA, IS FAMOUS FOR ITS STILT FISHERMEN, WHO CATCH FISH USING A HANDLINE WHILE SITTING ON WOODEN POLES THAT JUT OUT FROM THE WATER. I USED TO BEG MY DAD TO PAY THE STILT FISHERMEN FOR ME TO HAVE A GO BUT HE NEVER GAVE IN TO ME. FAST FORWARD THIRTY YEARS AND MY CHANCE FINALLY ARRIVED. IT WASN'T EXACTLY HOW I PICTURED IT. GETTING ONTO THE STILT WAS HILARIOUS — I'M PROBABLY 30 KILOGRAMS (65 POUNDS) HEAVIER THAN ANY OF THE FISHERMEN WHO USE THE POLES DAILY. AS I SCALED THE POLE IT BENT BACKWARDS, THEN AS I LIFTED MY SARONG-CLAD LEG OVER THE CROSSBAR MY SARONG GOT CAUGHT ON IT, BUT I FINALLY SETTLED ONTO THE STILT AND EVEN MANAGED TO CATCH A FISH.

SERVES 4

10 herrings, scaled and cleaned
1 tablespoon roasted curry powder
salt, to taste
2 teaspoons ground black pepper, to taste
150 g (5 oz/1 cup) plain (all-purpose) flour
juice of 1 lime
2 litres (4 pt 4 fl oz) vegetable oil
1 head garlic, cloves unpeeled and bruised
10 dried red chillies
spicy Sri Lankan salad (see page 173), to serve

Place the herrings, curry powder, salt, pepper and flour in a bowl and toss to coat the fish well. Add the lime juice and toss again.

Heat the oil in a large deep-sided saucepan to 180°C (360°F) or until a cube of bread turns golden in 15 seconds. Once the oil is hot, add the 3–4 herrings, one by one, and deep-fry until crisp and golden. Remove with a slotted spoon and drain on paper towel. Fry the herrings in batches so the oil doesn't lose its heat and allow the oil to come back up to temperature before frying another batch. Set aside.

Deep-fry the garlic cloves and whole chillies in the same oil until crisp and golden. Remove with a slotted spoon and drain on paper towel.

To serve, place a few herrings on each plate, topped with the fried garlic and chilli along with some Sri Lankan salad.

DEVILLED TUNA

THIS IS A DELICIOUS SRI LANKAN DELICACY BEST EATEN WITH A STIFF SCOTCH OR LOCAL ARRACK, A SPIRIT DISTILLED FROM COCONUT JUICE.

SERVES 2

300 g (10½ oz) tuna fillet, cut into
   bite-sized pieces
1 teaspoon salt
1 teaspoon red chilli powder
1 sprig curry leaves, leaves picked, plus
   extra to serve
juice of 1 lime
2 tablespoons vegetable oil
1 onion, quartered
3 garlic cloves, finely chopped
2 leeks, washed and chopped
3 banana capsicum (peppers), chopped
2 long red chillies, finely chopped
2 green chillies, thinly sliced
salt and ground black pepper, to taste

SWEET AND SOUR SAUCE
60 ml (2 fl oz/3 tablespoons) tomato sauce (ketchup)
60 ml (2 fl oz/3 tablespoons) white vinegar

Place the tuna in a bowl with the salt, chilli powder, curry leaves and lime juice. Stir to coat the tuna and set aside to marinate for 10 minutes.

   To make the sweet and sour sauce, combine all of the ingredients and set aside until ready to use.

   Heat the oil in a wok over high heat. Once it is hot, add the onion, garlic and leeks and cook until fragrant and the onion is starting to turn translucent. Add the chillies and fry, stirring occasionally, for a few minutes.

   Add the tuna and toss to coat in the onion mixture. Stir in the sweet and sour sauce, cover and cook for a few minutes or until the tuna is just cooked. Season with salt and pepper.

BARBECUED MARINATED PRAWNS

THE BARBECUE IS A PLACE WHERE YOU CAN EXPERIMENT AND HAVE FUN. IT IS A COMMUNAL WAY TO COOK AND A GREAT PLACE TO HAVE A FEW BEERS AND A CHAT WITH MATES. WHEN I WAS IN SRI LANKA, I COULDN'T RESIST TRYING THE LOCALLY-MADE CREAMY AND SLIGHTLY SOUR BUFFALO CURD IN A DRESSING FOR PRAWNS. I'VE SUBSTITUTED YOGHURT HERE; IT WORKS AS A TENDERISER AND ALSO ADDS A LOVELY SOURNESS TO THE PRAWNS.

SERVES 6

1.5 kg (3 lb 5 oz) prawns (shrimp), shelled
   and deveined with tails intact
1 dried red chilli, chopped
3 sprigs curry leaves, leaves picked
2 cm (¾ inch) piece of ginger, finely chopped
2 tablespoons fish sauce
1 tablespoon oyster sauce
3 spring onions (scallions), chopped
150 g (5 oz) yoghurt
1 French shallot, finely chopped
2 small green chillies, chopped
2 garlic cloves, thinly sliced
salt, to taste

Place the prawns with the dried chilli, curry leaves, ginger, fish sauce, oyster sauce and spring onion in a large bowl and combine well. Set aside for 10 minutes.

Place the yoghurt, shallot, chilli and garlic in a bowl, season with salt and stir to combine. Divide between two bowls and add the prawns to one bowl. Set aside to marinate for 10 minutes.

Preheat a barbecue hotplate to high. Cook the prawns on each side until just cooked through.

Toss the prawns in the remaining yoghurt mixture and serve.

BARBECUED TREVALLY WITH SAMBAL BAJAK

I WAS INSPIRED TO CREATE THIS DISH USING THE LOCAL FISH FROM MAKASSAR HARBOUR IN INDONESIA. GIANT WOODEN PHINISI BOATS, WHICH ARE USED TO TRANSPORT ANYTHING FROM LIVE PRODUCE TO CEMENT ACROSS THE INDONESIAN ARCHIPELAGO AND BEYOND, DOMINATE THE HARBOUR. TREVALLY IS SUCH A GREAT FISH TO BARBECUE. IT HAS FIRM WHITE FLESH AND TASTES SWEET.

SERVES 6

100 ml (3½ fl oz) cold-pressed extra virgin coconut oil (see glossary)
2 long red chillies, finely chopped
2 whole trevally (about 2 kg/4 lb 6 oz each), scaled and cleaned
thinly sliced spring onion (scallion), to serve
bean sprouts, to serve
lime wedges, to serve
sambal bajak (see page 181), to serve

Gently warm the coconut oil, add the chopped chilli, remove from the heat and leave to infuse for 30 minutes

Using a sharp knife, score the fish on both sides making sure the incisions do not go all the way through to the bone.

Light a charcoal barbecue and make sure the coals have burned down so there is no flame or preheat a regular barbecue to high. Brush the fish on both sides with the coconut and chilli oil and grill for about 6 minutes each side, basting the fish when you turn it. The cooking time will vary depending on the thickness of the fish. To check whether the fish is cooked, press it lightly just below the head and if it gives, then the fish is done.

Place on a large platter, scatter with the spring onion, chilli and bean sprouts and serve with the lime wedges and sambal alongside.

Salads and Condiments

FILIPINO SALAD WITH TINAWON RICE

THIS IS A DISPLAY OF THE FRESH VEGETABLES AVAILABLE FROM THE AMAZING BANAUE REGION OF THE PHILIPPINES. NESTLED IN THE HILLS OF NORTHERN LUZON, THE TOWN REMINDS ME OF THE BEAUTIFUL HILL STATIONS AROUND THE INDIAN–HIMALAYAN REGION. THE VARIETY OF RICE GROWN HERE, CALLED TINAWON, IS VERY RARE AND HAS A NUTTY TASTE. THE RICE PADDIES OF BANAUE ARE WORLD HERITAGE LISTED; BUILT ON THE EDGE OF THE MOUNTAINS, IT IS SAID THAT IF YOU LAID ALL THE TERRACES END-TO-END THEY WOULD STRETCH AROUND THE GLOBE. THE PEOPLE ARE WEATHERED FROM THE HARSH CLIMATE BUT ARE STILL VERY FIT AS THEY ARE CONSTANTLY WALKING UP AND DOWN THE HUNDREDS OF STAIRWAYS AROUND THE TOWN.

SERVES 6

200 g (7 oz) okra, trimmed
½ bunch snake (yard-long) beans
250 g (9 oz) sweet potato tops, leaves picked (optional)
250 g (9 oz) water spinach (kangkung) (see glossary), leaves picked
1 eggplant (aubergine) (about 600 g/1 lb 5 oz)
400 g (14 oz) white radish, peeled and cut into 5 cm x 1 cm (2 x ⅜ inch) sticks
300 g (10½ oz) green mango, peeled and cut into 1 cm (½ inch) thick strips
250 g (9 oz) ripe tomatoes, peeled, seeds removed and cut into petals
2 salted duck eggs (see glossary) or hard-boiled eggs, peeled and halved
sautéed shrimp paste dressing (see page 188), to serve
peanut sauce (see page 180), to serve
steamed tinawon rice or other nutty rice (see page 219), to serve

Steam the okra, snake beans, sweet potato tops (if using) and water spinach for 3 minutes, then plunge into iced water to refresh. Drain and set aside.

Grill the eggplant over a charcoal barbecue or a gas flame, turning occasionally, until the skin is blackened and charred all over. When cool enough to handle, peel and discard the blackened skin. Slice the flesh.

Place all of the vegetables and the egg on a large serving platter, ensuring all of the colours complement each other. Serve the sauces separately for dipping, and also bowls of rice.

From left to right: papaya salad (see page 167) and star fruit salad (see page 167).

PAPAYA SALAD

SPICY AND TASTY, THIS IS SIMILAR TO A THAI PAPAYA SALAD. CHOOSE A GREEN BUT MATURE PAPAYA, IN WHICH THE INSIDE HAS STARTED TO TURN RED BUT THE FLESH IS STILL HARD. SERVE WITH SEARED WAHOO, WITH SNAKE BEANS (SEE PAGE 145).

SERVES 6 (PICTURED PAGE 164)

1 green but mature papaya, peeled
2 red bird's eye chillies
1 tablespoon soft brown or grated palm sugar (jaggery)
2 garlic cloves
50 ml (1¾ fl oz) fish sauce, or to taste
juice of 1 lime

Peel the papaya. Using a vegetable peeler or knife, cut the papaya into long thin strips and place in a bowl. Discard the seeds.

Place the chilli, sugar, garlic and fish sauce in a mortar and pestle and grind to a coarse paste. Add the lime juice and adjust with a little more fish sauce if necessary. Just before serving, add the dressing to the papaya and toss to combine.

STAR FRUIT SALAD

CHOOSE STAR FRUIT THAT IS YELLOW. THE PURPOSE OF THIS SALAD IS TO ADD A SWEET AND SOUR COMPONENT TO A GRILLED PIECE OF FISH (SUCH AS THE GRILLED YELLOWTAIL WITH CASSAVA RICE ON PAGE 139, FOR EXAMPLE) OR YOU CAN USE AS A CONDIMENT FOR A CURRY.

SERVES 6 (PICTURED PAGE 165)

4 small star fruit, thinly sliced
6 small green chillies, finely chopped
juice of 2 limes
½ teaspoon salt
½ teaspoon pepper

Combine all of the ingredients in a bowl and set aside until ready to serve.

GOTU KOLA SAMBAL

IN SRI LANKA, *GOTU KOLA* (WHICH IS MORE COMMONLY KNOWN AS PENNYWORT) IS LOVED BY ALL FOR ITS SLIGHTLY BITTER FLAVOUR BUT ALSO ITS HEALTH AND AYURVEDIC PROPERTIES. IN THE MORNING ON THE WAY TO THE FISH MARKETS, LADIES SELL A HOT RICE PORRIDGE WITH GOTU KOLA JUICE IN IT — IT GIVES YOU ENERGY TO GET THROUGH THE DAY AND TASTES LOVELY. IT IS USUALLY SERVED WITH A CHUNK OF PALM SUGAR. THIS RAW SAMBAL MADE WITH GOTU KOLA IS SO TASTY AND FITS IN PERFECTLY WITH A MOUTHFUL OF CURRY. YOU CAN REPLACE THE GOTU KOLA WITH FLAT-LEAF (ITALIAN) PARSLEY IF YOU CAN'T FIND IT AT AN ASIAN GREENGROCER.

MAKES 1 CUP (PICTURED PAGE 174)

2 cups picked gotu kola (pennywort) leaves
80 g (3 oz) freshly grated coconut
½ onion, finely chopped
2 small green chillies, finely chopped
1 teaspoon Maldive fish flakes (see glossary)
juice of 1 lime
½ teaspoon salt
½ teaspoon cracked black pepper

Finely shred the gotu kola leaves using a sharp knife. Combine with the remaining ingredients and mix well. Serve immediately.

BEETROOT SALAD

I LOVE THE COLOUR AND FLAVOUR OF BEETROOT. THIS IS A VIBRANT SALAD WITH A HINT OF SPICE.

SERVES 4 (PICTURED OPPOSITE)

1 × 400 g (14 oz) tin sliced beetroot (beets), drained
1 tomato, finely diced
1 onion, finely diced
½ green capsicum (pepper), finely diced
1 tablespoon lime juice
1 garlic clove, minced with a pinch of salt
1 teaspoon grated palm sugar (jaggery)
salt, to taste
1 tablespoon ground black pepper

Arrange the beetroot on a serving platter and scatter over the tomato, onion and capsicum. Combine the lime juice, garlic and sugar and stir until the sugar is dissolved. Season with the salt and pepper, then drizzle over the salad.

beetroot salad

BEAN SALAD

FRESH AND LIGHT, THIS IS A GREAT ACCOMPANIMENT TO A PIECE OF GRILLED FISH OR RED MEAT (SUCH AS THE BARBECUED ISLAND BEEF WITH SALSA VERDE ON PAGE 100).

SERVES 6

200 g (7 oz) green beans, trimmed
3 sprigs flat-leaf (Italian) parsley, leaves picked
2 tablespoons capers in brine, drained and chopped
50 ml (1¾ fl oz) olive oil
salt and ground black pepper, to taste

Blanch the beans in a saucepan of boiling salted water, then drain and refresh in iced water. Drain again, combine with the parsley, capers and oil. Season with salt and pepper and set aside.

CUCUMBER SALAD

A COOLING SALAD AND GREAT ACCOMPANIMENT TO A HOT CURRY.

SERVES 4

1 large cucumber
1 tomato
½ green capsicum (pepper)
½ cup fresh pineapple chunks
2 tablespoons white sugar
1 tablespoon white vinegar
pinch of red chilli powder
salt and ground black pepper, to taste
lime juice, to taste

Peel the cucumber and cut the flesh into small cubes. Cut the tomato, capsicum and pineapple (if the chunks are too big) into small cubes. Place all of the ingredients in a bowl, season with salt, pepper and lime juice and mix well.

SKY POTATO SALAD

THESE BEAUTIFUL POTATOES DO NOT GROW IN THE GROUND BUT ON A VINE, HENCE THEIR NAME. YOU CAN SUBSTITUTE ANY POTATO OR SWEET POTATO (YAM). THIS SALAD IS AN EXCELLENT ACCOMPANIMENT TO THE BARBECUED ISLAND BEEF WITH SALSA VERDE (SEE PAGE 100).

SERVES 6

1 kg (2 lb 3 oz) sky potatoes or red potatoes,
   cut into 2 cm (¾ inch) cubes
1 onion, finely diced
4 spring onions (scallions) (white part only), thinly sliced
50 ml (1¾ fl oz) lime juice
1 garlic clove, minced with a pinch of salt
1 tablespoon white sugar
1 teaspoon cracked black pepper
100 ml (3½ fl oz) olive oil

Place the potato in a saucepan of cold salted water over high heat, bring to the boil and cook for 15 minutes or until tender. Drain well.

   Combine the warm potato with the remaining ingredients and gently mix.

SPICY SRI LANKAN SALAD

CRISP, SPICY, TANGY AND CRUNCHY, THIS SALAD IS PERFECT WITH GRILLED FISH (SUCH AS THE CRISP HERRINGS ON PAGE 151) OR BEEF.

SERVES 6

1 large red onion, thinly sliced
3 green chillies, finely chopped
4 ripe tomatoes, sliced
1 cucumber, sliced
2 teaspoons Maldive fish flakes (see glossary)
juice of 1 lime
salt and ground black pepper, to taste

Combine all of the ingredients in a large bowl, toss well and set aside until ready to serve.

COCONUT HEART SALAD

WHEN A COCONUT GERMINATES, THE CENTRE OF THE NUT FILLS WITH A SOFT BUT CRUNCHY APPLE-LIKE MASS. IT IS ABSOLUTELY BEAUTIFUL TO EAT. IT MAY BE DIFFICULT TO FIND, SO YOU CAN SUBSTITUTE PEELED APPLE INSTEAD.

SERVES 4

2 coconut hearts or 1 Granny Smith apple, thinly sliced
3 vine-ripened tomatoes, thinly sliced
juice of 1 lime
50 ml (1¾ fl oz) olive oil
salt and ground black pepper, to taste

Arrange the coconut heart and tomato in alternate slices on a platter. Dress with the lime juice and oil and season with salt and pepper.

From left to right: gotu kola sambal (see page 168),
coconut sambal (see page 176), cucumber sambal (see page 176),
carrot sambal (see page 177), and tomato sambal (see page 177).

COCONUT SAMBAL

ALSO KNOWN AS POL SAMBAL, THIS IS SERVED WITH NEARLY EVERY SRI LANKAN MEAL, ESPECIALLY STRING HOPPERS (SEE PAGE 205). FRESH COCONUT SHOULD BE USED BECAUSE DRY IS JUST NOT AS JUICY. WHEN WE FIRST ARRIVED IN AUSTRALIA IN 1979 IT WAS DIFFICULT TO GET A FRESH COCONUT SO WE USED TO RECONSTITUTE DESICCATED COCONUT WITH WARM WATER. IT'S NOT AS GOOD AS FRESH, BUT IT'S ACCEPTABLE. THE SAMBAL IS SUPPOSED TO BE AN ORANGEY RED DUE TO THE PAPRIKA.

MAKES 2 CUPS (PICTURED PAGE 174)

1 teaspoon black peppercorns
1 tablespoon Maldive fish flakes (see glossary)
60 g (2 oz) bombay onion (see glossary) or
    French shallots, roughly chopped
2 teaspoons red chilli powder
1 teaspoon Spanish paprika
1 large fresh coconut, flesh grated (see note)
juice of 1 lime
salt, to taste

Using a large mortar and pestle, grind the peppercorns and fish flakes. Add the onion and grind well. Add the chilli and paprika and grind to a coarse paste. Add the coconut and pound together until thoroughly combined. Add the lime juice, a little at a time, tasting to check it is not too sour, then season with salt.

Note *You can substitute 100 g (3½ oz) desiccated coconut combined with 100 ml (3½ fl oz) water.*

CUCUMBER SAMBAL

THIS IS A COOLING SALAD TO PAIR WITH SEAFOOD. SERVE WITH PAN-ROASTED PAINTED CRAYFISH AND FRIED ANCHOVIES (SEE PAGE 142).

SERVES 6 (PICTURED PAGE 175)

1 large telegraph (long) cucumber, peeled, shaved into
    ribbons using a vegetable peeler, core discarded
1 teaspoon chilli flakes
60 ml (2 fl oz/3 tablespoons) tamarind water (see note)
juice of 2 lemons
1 tablespoon grated palm sugar (jaggery)
3 red Asian shallots or ½ red onion, finely diced
2 garlic cloves, minced with a pinch of salt
3 dried squid, finely shredded
2 tablespoons freshly grated coconut
60 ml (2 fl oz/3 tablespoons) lime juice

Combine all of the ingredients in a bowl and set aside for at least 5 minutes for the flavours to combine and infuse.

Note *To make tamarind water, place 50 g (1¾ oz) tamarind pulp in a heatproof bowl and pour over 150 ml (5 fl oz) of boiling water. Allow to cool, then mix together to combine well. Strain through a fine mesh sieve, extracting as much liquid as possible. Discard the solids. Makes 100 ml (3½ fl oz) tamarind water.*

CARROT SAMBAL

THIS PARTNERS WELL WITH PORK (TRY IT WITH THE TEA COUNTRY PORK CURRY ON PAGE 68) OR SEAFOOD, AND THE COCONUT ADDS A NICE DEPTH AND RICHNESS.

SERVES 6 (PICTURED PAGE 175)

1 carrot, cut into julienne
2 green chillies, finely shredded
1 small onion, finely diced
juice of 1 lime
1 garlic clove, very finely chopped
½ cup freshly grated coconut
1 sprig curry leaves, finely shredded
2 teaspoons Maldive fish flakes (see glossary)
salt and ground black pepper, to taste

Combine all of the ingredients in a small bowl and set aside until ready to serve.

TOMATO SAMBAL

A TERRIFIC CONDIMENT FOR A CURRY. ADD MORE CHILLI IF YOU WANT IT HOTTER BUT KEEP IN MIND HOW HOT THE CURRY IS YOU'RE SERVING IT WITH — IT'S SUPPOSED TO BE REFRESHING. I LIKE TO SERVE THIS WITH THE PRAWN AND SWEET POTATO ROLLS (SEE PAGE 16).

SERVES 3 (PICTURED PAGE 175)

3 ripe tomatoes, quartered
1 onion, thinly sliced
2 green chillies, finely chopped
1 garlic clove, finely chopped
½ teaspoon Maldive fish flakes (see glossary)
juice of 1 lime
salt and ground black pepper, to taste

Combine all of the ingredients in a small bowl and set aside until ready to serve.

From left to right: sambal terasi (see page 180), peanut sauce (see page 180), sambal bajak (see page 181), bitter gourd sambal (see page 181), sambal olek (see page 182), and coconut cream sauce (see page 182).

SAMBAL TERASI

THIS IS A VERY HOT SAMBAL. TERASI IS THE INDONESIAN VERSION OF SHRIMP PASTE, AND ALTHOUGH THE SMELL AND RAW TASTE IS VERY STRONG, ONCE COOKED IT ADDS THE FLAVOUR OF INDONESIA TO YOUR DISHES. CANDLENUTS ADD A RICH FLAVOUR AND ALSO ASSIST IN THE THICKENING OF THE SAMBAL, BUT THEY MUST BE COOKED FIRST, OTHERWISE THEY WILL GIVE YOU A STOMACH ACHE. ENJOY THIS SAMBAL WITH CRISPY DRIED FISH (SEE PAGE 147).

MAKES ½ CUP (PICTURED PAGE 178)

6 red bird's eye chillies, chopped
5 candlenuts (see glossary), chopped
3 red Asian shallots, chopped
2 cm (¾ inch) piece of ginger, chopped
2 garlic cloves, chopped
2 tablespoons grated palm sugar (jaggery)
2 teaspoons fermented shrimp paste (terasi)
1 teaspoon ground turmeric
100 ml (3½ fl oz) tamarind water (see note right)
juice of 1 lime
60 ml (2 fl oz/3 tablespoons) palm oil (see glossary)

Using a large mortar and pestle, grind the chilli, candlenuts, shallot, ginger, garlic, sugar, shrimp paste and turmeric to a coarse paste. Add the tamarind water and lime juice and grind until well combined.

Heat the palm oil in a wok over medium heat. When hot, add the paste and stir-fry for 10 minutes until thick and pulpy. Remove from the heat and cool.

PEANUT SAUCE

THIS FILIPINO-STYLE PEANUT SAUCE IS MADE FOR GRILLED VEGETABLES. USE IN THE FILIPINO SALAD WITH TINAWON RICE (SEE PAGE 163).

MAKES 2 CUPS (PICTURED PAGE 178)

100 ml (3½ fl oz) peanut oil
200 g (7 oz) raw peanuts
2 garlic cloves
4 French shallots, chopped
1 teaspoon roasted Filipino shrimp paste
½ teaspoon red chilli powder
2 teaspoons soft brown sugar
1 tablespoon dark soy sauce
1 tablespoon tamarind water (see note)
500 ml (17 fl oz/2 cups) water

Heat the oil in a wok over medium heat, add the peanuts and cook until golden. Remove with a slotted spoon and drain on paper towel. Once cool, grind the peanuts in a small food processor until finely chopped.

Using a mortar and pestle, crush the garlic, shallot and shrimp paste until smooth. Heat 1 teaspoon of the peanut cooking oil in a wok over medium heat, add the garlic paste and cook, stirring constantly, for 2 minutes or until fragrant.

Add the chilli powder, sugar, soy sauce, tamarind water, water and peanuts, bring to the boil, then reduce the heat to low and simmer for 8–10 minutes or until the sauce has thickened. Remove from the heat and serve warm.

Note *To make tamarind water, place 50 g (1¾ oz) tamarind pulp in a heatproof bowl and pour over 150 ml (5 fl oz) of boiling water. Allow to cool, then mix together to combine well. Strain through a fine mesh sieve, extracting as much liquid as possible. Discard the solids. Makes 100 ml (3½ fl oz) tamarind water.*

SAMBAL BAJAK

THIS IS INDONESIA'S FAVOURITE SAMBAL, AROMATIC AND PERFECTLY SUITED TO BARBECUED MEATS AND FISH. IT HAS A NICE HEAT TO IT.

MAKES 2 CUPS (PICTURED PAGE 179)

4–6 red or green bird's eye chillies, coarsely chopped
4 spring onions (scallions) (white part only), coarsely chopped
30 g (1 oz) peeled galangal (see glossary), coarsely chopped
30 g (1 oz) peeled ginger, coarsely chopped
2 kaffir lime leaves
4 garlic cloves
2 teaspoons lime juice
1 teaspoon salt
1 tablespoon grated palm sugar (jaggery)
2 teaspoons fermented shrimp paste (terasi) (see glossary)
1 tablespoon palm oil (see glossary)
100 ml (3½ fl oz) tamarind water (see note opposite)

Using a large mortar and pestle or a spice grinder, grind the chilli, spring onion, galangal, ginger, lime leaves, garlic, lime juice and salt to a coarse paste. Add the sugar and shrimp paste and grind until well combined.

Heat the oil in a wok over medium heat. When hot, add the paste and stir-fry for 2–3 minutes or until fragrant.

Stir in the tamarind water and simmer until reduced by half. Remove from the heat and cool. Store in an airtight jar in the refrigerator for up to 7 days.

BITTER GOURD SAMBAL

I LOVE THE BITTERNESS OF THIS VEGETABLE BUT IT IS AN ACQUIRED TASTE. WHEN YOU HEAT THE OIL, ENSURE IT DOES NOT EXCEED 160°C (320°F), SO THAT THE GOURD WILL RETAIN A NICE GREEN COLOUR.

SERVES 6 (PICTURED PAGE 179)

450 g (1 lb) bitter gourd (see glossary)
¼ cup fine salt
vegetable oil, for deep-frying
2 small green chillies, chopped
1 onion, very thinly sliced
1 teaspoon Maldive fish flakes (see glossary)
lime juice, to taste
½ teaspoon cracked black pepper

Remove the seeds from the gourd without cutting it in half. Using a very sharp knife or mandolin, slice the gourd into very thin slices. Place in a bowl, add the salt and massage it into the gourd. Set aside for 10 minutes. Place the gourd in a large strainer and wash it two or three times to ensure all of the salt is rinsed off. Pat the gourd dry with a tea towel.

Heat the oil in a deep-sided saucepan until 160°C (320°F) or until a cube of bread turns golden in 30–35 seconds. Deep-fry the gourd, in batches, until crisp but retaining its colour — it is cooked when there are only a few bubbles coming out of the gourd. Remove with a slotted spoon and drain on paper towel.

Combine the gourd and remaining ingredients in a bowl, season with salt and mix well. If it's too bitter, add more lime juice. Set aside until ready to serve.

Sambal olek

THIS CONDIMENT IS IN EVERYONE'S PANTRY IN INDONESIA. IT CAN BE SERVED HOT OR COLD, AND IS AN IDEAL SIDE TO JUST ABOUT ANY DISH.

MAKES 1 CUP (PICTURED PAGE 179)

2 cm (¾ inch) piece of ginger, chopped
2 garlic cloves, chopped
1 stick lemongrass (white part only), finely chopped
6–8 red bird's eye chillies or to taste, chopped
finely grated zest of 1 lime
50 ml (1¾ fl oz) white vinegar
coarse salt, to taste
110 g (4 oz/½ cup) white sugar

Using a large mortar and pestle, grind the ginger, garlic and lemongrass together. Add the chilli and half of the lime zest and grind the ingredients together. Add the vinegar, which will add sourness and bring out many of the flavours in the sambal. Add a pinch of salt and continue grinding. The salt will assist in breaking down the ingredients. Taste the mix to ensure you are happy with the combination of sour, salty and hot flavours. Add more of the ingredients to balance the taste as necessary.

Place the sambal in a small frying pan over high heat, being careful not to let the flames come up around the sides of the pan (as this will burn the edges of the sambal). Stir as it heats up.

Add the sugar, which will caramelise the sambal and bring the flavours together.

When the solids start to break down and the mixture starts to thicken, it is almost done. Add the remaining lime zest and cook for 1½ minutes to keep the lime flavour fresh, but not raw, then reduce the heat to medium and cook for 10 minutes or until the mixture is pulpy. Serve hot or cold. Store in an airtight jar in the refrigerator for up to 7 days.

Coconut cream sauce

AVOID TINNED COCONUT CREAM AS PASTEURISATION AFFECTS THE FLAVOUR. SERVE WITH WHOLE FISH UMU AT HOME (SEE PAGE 148).

MAKES ABOUT 1 LITRE (34 FL OZ/4 CUPS) (PICTURED PAGE 179)

1 litre (34 fl oz/4 cups) first-extract coconut milk
   or coconut cream (see note)
1 onion, finely diced
1 vine-ripened tomato, seeds removed and finely diced
3–4 small green chillies, finely chopped
salt and ground black pepper, to taste

Combine the coconut cream, onion, tomato and chilli in a bowl, season with salt and pepper and mix well.

Note *To make first-extract coconut milk (also known as coconut cream), crack a coconut with the back of a large cleaver. Reserve the coconut water as it drains out. For this recipe you will need 1 litre (34 fl oz/4 cups) of coconut water; if you don't have enough, top up with filtered water. Scrape out the white flesh and trim off the brown membrane. Grate the flesh with a hand-grater or in a food processor. Place the grated flesh and the reserved coconut water in a blender and, using the pulse action, process until everything is well combined and the flesh is soft. Line a sieve with muslin (cheesecloth) and place over a bowl. Pour in the blended coconut, then gather the sides of the muslin and squeeze to extract as much liquid as possible from the flesh. This is the first-extract coconut milk or coconut cream. (You can also make second extract coconut milk to use for another recipe. Simply repeat the process using the same coconut flesh, using filtered water if coconut water is not available.)*

ACHARA

ACHARA IS A FILIPINO PICKLE THAT CAN BE MADE USING ANY TYPE OF VEGETABLE. THE MOST COMMON VARIATION USES GREEN PAPAYA. IN SRI LANKA, THIS IS KNOWN AS ACHARU AND IT CAN BE AS SPICY AS YOU LIKE. ACHARA ALSO CAN BE USED TO PICKLE SEAFOOD OR SEMI-COOK IT.

MAKES 3 CUPS

500 ml (17 fl oz/2 cups) chilli cane vinegar (see glossary)
500 g (1 lb 2 oz) white sugar
1 small white radish (daikon), peeled and cut into julienne
1 carrot, cut into julienne
1 small green papaya, peeled and cut into julienne
4 long red chillies, seeds removed and cut into julienne
50 g (1¾ oz) ginger, cut into julienne
1 garlic clove, blanched and bruised

Place the vinegar and sugar in a saucepan over low heat, stir until the sugar dissolves and bring to the boil.

Remove from the heat and leave to cool.

Add the remaining ingredients, stir to combine well and leave for at least 10 minutes. Drain, discarding the liquid, and refrigerate until ready to serve.

RED ONION SOUBISE

SOUBISE IS A RICH AND VELVETY SAUCE THAT IS PERFECT WITH MEAT AND FISH. USING A GOOD SAUTERNE OR STICKY DESSERT WINE WILL ENHANCE THE FLAVOUR AND GIVE IT SOME DEPTH. USING RED ONIONS WILL GIVE THE SAUCE A BEAUTIFUL PINK TINGE AND IT WILL ALSO BE A LOT MILDER THAN USING BROWN ONIONS OR FRENCH SHALLOTS. I LIKE TO SERVE IT WITH THE SEARED WAHOO, SNAKE BEANS AND PAPAYA SALAD (SEE PAGE 145).

MAKES 2 CUPS (PICTURED PAGE 184)

4 red onions, chopped
100 ml (3½ fl oz) thin (pouring) cream
200 ml (7 fl oz) dessert wine or sweet riesling
salt, to taste

Place the onion, cream, wine and a pinch of salt in a heavy-based saucepan over high heat and bring to the boil.

Reduce the heat to medium, cover the saucepan and cook for 20 minutes or until pulpy. You will need to stir the mixture every 5 minutes to prevent it sticking and burning.

Transfer to a blender and purée until smooth. Strain through a fine mesh sieve and set aside until needed.

From left to right: red onion soubise (see page 183), black pepper and curry leaf sauce (see page 186), mango salsa (see page 186), harissa (see page 187) and tomato chilli jam (see page 187).

BLACK PEPPER AND CURRY LEAF SAUCE

THIS SAUCE IS SO VERSATILE. YOU CAN CRUST SEAFOOD IN SALT AND PEPPER, THEN COAT IT WITH THE HOT SAUCE; RUB IT ON MEAT FOR BARBECUING OR SERVE IT AS A DIPPING SAUCE — IT'S GREAT WITH ANYTHING, BUT ESPECIALLY THE GRILLED BANANA PRAWNS (SEE PAGE 144).

MAKES 3 CUPS (PICTURED PAGE 184)

100 ml (3½ fl oz) vegetable oil
1 sprig curry leaves, leaves picked
6 bombay onions (see glossary) or French shallots, very finely chopped
5 cm (2 inch) piece of ginger, thinly sliced
3 garlic cloves, finely chopped
3 long red chillies, finely chopped
150 g (5 oz) butter, chopped
1 tablespoon white sugar
1 tablespoon fish sauce
1 tablespoon light soy sauce
1 tablespoon dark soy sauce
1 tablespoon oyster sauce
3 teaspoons ground black pepper

Heat the oil in a heavy-based saucepan over high heat, add the curry leaves, onion, ginger, garlic and chilli and cook until the onion is translucent.

Add the butter and reduce the heat immediately so as not to burn the butter.

When the butter has melted, add the sugar, fish sauce, soy sauce, oyster sauce and pepper and stir to combine. Reduce the heat to low, cover and simmer, stirring occasionally, for about 45 minutes or until the sauce has reduced and is thick.

MANGO SALSA

EVERYONE LOVES MANGOES IN SEASON. HERE'S WHAT TO DO WITH THEM WHEN YOU HAVE TOO MANY.

MAKES 2 CUPS (PICTURED PAGE 184)

2 green but mature mangoes, peeled and cut into 2 cm (¾ inch) cubes
2 tablespoons finely chopped French shallot
1 small onion, diced
1 spring onion (scallion), thinly sliced
1 small red chilli, seeds removed and chopped
½ garlic clove, minced
juice of 1 lime
1 tablespoon cane sugar
salt and ground black pepper, to taste

Combine all of the ingredients in a bowl and mix well. Check for flavour and balance. The salsa should be sweet, sour and spicy.

HARISSA

HOT AND SPICY, THIS IS GREAT WITH A BOWL OF MUSSELS OR IN A SOUP, OR JUST SPREAD ON BREAD.

MAKES 1 CUP (PICTURED PAGE 185)

3 red capsicums (peppers), seeds removed
   and finely chopped
½ onion, finely chopped
6 garlic cloves, bruised
250 ml (8 ½ fl oz/1 cup) vegetable oil
1 tablespoon hot paprika
1 tablespoon ground cumin
2 teaspoons ground turmeric
1 teaspoon red chilli powder

Preheat the oven to 180°C (360°F/Gas 4).

Place the capsicum, onion, garlic and oil in a roasting tray, season with the spices, cover with foil and roast for 40 minutes or until soft.

Transfer the contents of the tray to a blender and blend until a smooth purée. Store in an airtight jar in the refrigerator for up to 7 days.

TOMATO CHILLI JAM

I ALWAYS HAVE A JAR OF THIS IN MY FRIDGE. IT COMES IN HANDY ON SO MANY OCCASIONS. FOR MANY YEARS THIS WAS A STAPLE ON MANY RESTAURANT MENUS BECAUSE IT IS SO TASTY AND VIBRANTLY RED IN COLOUR.

MAKES 2 CUPS (PICTURED PAGE 185)

5 large ripe tomatoes
3 long red chillies, roughly chopped
2 garlic cloves, finely chopped
240 g (8 ½ oz) soft brown sugar
125 ml (4 fl oz/½ cup) white wine
1 teaspoon finely grated ginger
2 tablespoons soy sauce
½ teaspoon sea salt

Blend the tomato, chilli and garlic in a blender until smooth.

Place in a saucepan, add the sugar, wine, ginger, soy sauce and salt and bring to the boil over high heat.

Reduce the heat to a simmer and cook for 30–35 minutes or until thickened. Store in an airtight jar in the refrigerator for up to 7 days.

KARE KARE SAUCE

THIS SAUCE EPITOMISES PINOY CUISINE. THE ADDITION OF PEANUT BUTTER MAKES IT OUT OF THIS WORLD. SERVE WITH BEEF OR CHICKEN (SEE PAGE 104).

MAKES ABOUT ¾ CUP

125 ml (4 fl oz/½ cup) vegetable oil
80 ml (3 fl oz/⅓ cup) annatto oil (see glossary)
3 garlic cloves, minced
1 small onion, diced
1 tablespoon crunchy peanut butter
1 tablespoon smooth peanut butter
1 litre (34 fl oz/4 cups) beef stock
¼ cup ground toasted rice

Heat the vegetable oil and annatto oil in a large saucepan or wok over medium heat, add the garlic and onion and cook until golden. Add the peanut butters and reserved stock and simmer until reduced by half. Add the toasted rice and stir until thick and gelatinous. Remove from the heat and keep warm.

SAUTÉED SHRIMP PASTE DRESSING

STINKY BUT TASTY, THIS DRESSING IS LOVELY ONCE IT'S COOKED OUT, SO DON'T JUDGE IT UNTIL IT'S READY. IT CONTAINS A CLASSIC PINOY TWIST — PORK. THE FILIPINOS LOVE THEIR PORK, SO DON'T BE SURPRISED IF IT TURNS UP IN THE MOST UNUSUAL PLACES. THIS IS GREAT IN THE FILIPINO SALAD WITH TINAWON RICE (SEE PAGE 163).

MAKES 1 CUP

50 ml (1¾ fl oz) vegetable oil
4 garlic cloves, minced
80 g (3 oz) white onion, finely chopped
120 g (4 oz) pork belly with fat, cut into
    5 cm (2 inch) pieces
350 g (12 oz) tomatoes, seeds removed and chopped
60 g (2 oz) fermented shrimp paste (see glossary)
3 red bird's eye chillies, chopped
1 teaspoon white sugar

Heat the oil in a wok over medium heat, add the garlic and onion and cook for 5–6 minutes or until soft. Add the pork, and cook, stirring constantly, for 5 minutes or until the pork is cooked.
    Add the tomato and cook for 5 minutes or until mushy.
    Add the shrimp paste, reduce the heat to low and stir for 5 minutes.
    Stir in the sugar, remove from the heat and cool to room temperature.

AIOLI

USE IN THE CHILLED KING PRAWNS WITH AIOLI AND LEMON (SEE PAGE 26).

MAKES ABOUT 1 ½ CUPS

2 egg yolks
2 confit garlic cloves (see note)
1 tablespoon Dijon mustard
200 ml (7 fl oz) vegetable oil
25 ml (¾ fl oz) extra virgin olive oil
1 tablespoon warm water
juice of 1 lemon
salt and ground black pepper, to taste

Place the egg yolks, garlic and mustard in a food processor and blend until well combined. With the motor running, add the combined oils in a slow steady stream, gradually increasing the flow of oil until it is all incorporated. Transfer to a bowl, stir in the water and lemon juice and season with salt and pepper. Press a piece of plastic wrap onto the surface and store in the refrigerator for up to 7 days.

Note *To confit garlic, place whole peeled garlic cloves in a small baking dish, add just enough olive oil to cover and cook in a preheated 150°C (300°F/Gas 2) oven for 40 minutes or until the garlic is soft and pulpy. Transfer to a glass jar and store in the refrigerator.*

SALSA VERDE

THIS CLASSIC CONDIMENT IS GREAT WITH ANYTHING BUT I LOVE IT ON BARBECUED MEAT (SUCH AS THE BARBECUED ISLAND BEEF ON PAGE 100).

MAKES 2 CUPS

½ bunch rocket (arugula) leaves
½ bunch Thai coriander (pointed cilantro), roots trimmed
¼ bunch peppermint, leaves picked
½ cup basil leaves
½ cup flat-leaf (Italian) parsley leaves
2 tablespoons capers in brine
2 sprigs thyme, leaves picked
3 garlic cloves
1 long green chilli
100 ml (3 ½ fl oz) olive oil
1 tablespoon lime juice
salt and ground black pepper, to taste

Place all of the ingredients in a blender and blend until well combined. Transfer to a bowl and set aside until some of the oil separates from the solids.

GINGER CHILLI SHALLOT SAUCE

THIS IS ANOTHER OF MY SECRET SAUCES REVEALED. SIMPLY POUR IT ONTO CHICKEN OR SEAFOOD TO COVER AND COOK IT IN THE SAUCE.

MAKES 1.5 LITRES (3 PT 3 FL OZ)

350 ml (12 fl oz) white wine
300 ml (10 fl oz) soy sauce
300 ml (10 fl oz) sweet chilli sauce
300 ml (10 fl oz) water
100 ml (3½ fl oz) sesame oil
150 g (5 oz) white sugar
¼ bunch spring onions (scallions), chopped
10 garlic cloves
3 long red chillies, finely chopped

Place all of the ingredients in a blender and blend for 1–2 minutes or until smooth. Do not strain. Store in an airtight container in the refrigerator for up to 2 weeks.

SESAME AND GOLDEN SYRUP DRESSING

CREATED YEARS AGO AT BLUE WATER GRILL IN BONDI BEACH, I DO NOT THINK THERE IS A BETTER SAUCE FOR OCTOPUS, GRILLED OR IN A SALAD. DON'T TASTE IT TOO MANY TIMES WHEN MAKING IT AS YOU WILL EVENTUALLY ONLY BE ABLE TO TASTE THE SESAME OIL AND NOTHING ELSE. USE IN THE OCTOPUS, SURF CLAMS AND UDON NOODLE SALAD (SEE PAGE 131).

MAKES ABOUT 1 ½ CUPS

100 g (3 ½ oz) golden syrup
100 ml (3 ½ fl oz) olive oil
75 ml (2 ½ fl oz) sesame oil
75 ml (2 ½ fl oz) balsamic vinegar
½ bunch coriander (cilantro), leaves and stalks chopped
1 bird's eye chilli, seeds removed and chopped

Whisk the golden syrup, oils and vinegar together in a bowl. Add the remaining ingredients and stir to combine. Set aside until needed and give it a good whisk before using.

COCONUT MILK GRAVY KIRI HODDI

When we first arrived in Sri Lanka I was a little cockney boy, not really used to curry for breakfast, lunch and dinner, so my grandmother always cooked this gravy for me. It tastes so good and is not spicy at all. This is the beginner curry eater's sauce. It is so tasty and perfect with string hoppers (see recipe on page 205).

MAKES ABOUT 3 CUPS

1 onion, thinly sliced
1 small green chilli, halved lengthways
4–6 curry leaves
2 cm (¾ inch) piece of pandan leaf
2 garlic cloves, thinly sliced
½ teaspoon ground turmeric
½ teaspoon fenugreek seeds
1 teaspoon Maldive fish flakes (see glossary) (optional)
1 teaspoon salt
250 ml (8½ fl oz/1 cup) water
500 ml (17 fl oz/2 cups) thick coconut milk
1 tablespoon lime juice

Place all of the ingredients, except the coconut milk and lime juice, in a heavy-based saucepan over low heat and simmer for 5 minutes or until the onion is soft.

Stirring constantly, add the coconut milk and continue to stir for 1–2 minutes. It is important to keep stirring to prevent the milk from coagulating. Do not let it boil.

Remove from the heat and add the salt and lime juice.

CANE VINEGAR DIP

Cane vinegar is coloured, infused with the bark of a special tree and fermented in giant earthenware vats. It is essential with Pinoy food. Use in the empanada special (see page 29).

MAKES ABOUT ½ CUP

100 ml (3½ fl oz) cane vinegar (sukang iloko) (see glossary)
3 red or green bird's eye chillies, finely chopped
1 small onion, finely chopped
1 garlic clove, thinly sliced

Combine all of the ingredients in a small bowl and set aside until needed.

SPRING ONION AND LIME DRESSING

THIS IS A GREAT VINAIGRETTE FOR RAW FISH OR A GRILLED FISH SALAD. TRY IT IN THE RAW TREVALLY SALAD WITH POMEGRANATE (SEE PAGE 128).

MAKES ABOUT ¾ CUP

juice and finely grated zest of 2 limes
1 tablespoon fish sauce
1 teaspoon soy sauce
50 g (1¾ oz) soft brown sugar
2 long red chillies, finely chopped
2 garlic cloves, minced
1 French shallot, finely chopped
1 bunch coriander (cilantro), roots only, minced
1 spring onion (scallion), finely chopped
ground black pepper, to taste

Place the lime juice, fish sauce, soy sauce and sugar in a bowl and stir to dissolve the sugar. Add the remaining ingredients, season with pepper and mix well. Set aside until needed.

CHILLI, LIME AND SEAWATER SAUCE

BASIC BUT PERFECT. THE ONLY THING YOU NEED HERE IS PRISTINE WATER FROM THE OCEAN THAT IS CRYSTAL CLEAR AND COMPLETELY FREE OF POLLUTANTS. WHEN I WAS IN FIJI, I USED TO GO FISHING AT NIGHT. I WOULD TAKE ONLY MY FISHING LINES, AND A LIME AND SOME FRESH CHILLI TO MAKE MY SUPPER. I USED TO BUILD A BIG FIRE ON THE BEACH AND AS I PULLED A FISH OUT OF THE WATER I THREW IT STRAIGHT INTO THE FLAMES — NO CLEANING OR SCALING, THE SCALES ACTUALLY PROTECTED THE FLESH — AND THE WHOLE FISH WOULD GO BLACK. I SIMPLY PEELED THE SKIN OFF AND THE SCALES WOULD COME OFF WITH IT, THEN I TOOK A PIECE OF THE JUICY FLESH AND DIPPED IT IN SEAWATER MIXED WITH LIME AND CHILLI. TRY THIS WITH THE COCONUT CRAB AND SEAFOOD PLATTER (SEE PAGE 136).

MAKES ¾ CUP

juice of 2 limes
150 ml (5 fl oz) fresh seawater or heavily salted water
3 small red or green chillies, finely chopped

Combine all of the ingredients in a bowl and set aside until needed.

CHILLI AND LIME SALT

THIS IS GREAT AS A DIP WITH GRILLED SEAFOOD (SUCH AS THE PAN-ROASTED PAINTED CRAYFISH AND FRIED ANCHOVIES ON PAGE 142).

MAKES ABOUT 2 GENEROUS TABLESPOONFULS

6 red bird's eye chillies, roughly chopped
1 tablespoon sea salt
squeeze of lime juice

Using a mortar and pestle, coarsely grind the chilli and salt together, then stir in the lime juice. Set aside until needed.

Roti, Rice and Accompaniments

ROTI

WHY BUY BREAD WHEN YOU CAN EASILY MAKE THESE BEAUTIFUL AND SIMPLE ROTI. THESE ARE MY DAD'S FAVOURITE TO MOP UP A MEAT CURRY.

MAKES 9–10

750 g (1 lb 10 oz/5 cups) plain (all-purpose) flour (see note),
   plus extra for dusting or atta flour (see glossary)
50 g (1¾ oz) ghee (see glossary)
pinch of salt
about 375 ml (12½ fl oz/1½ cups) water
vegetable oil or butter, for cooking
coconut sambal (see page 176), to serve

Place the flour, ghee and salt in a large bowl. Gradually add the water, a little at a time, using your hands to mix in and bring together to form a large ball of dough. It should not be too wet, but just wet enough to make it into a ball. If the dough is too dry, add a little more water. If the dough is too wet, add more flour.

Divide the dough into 9 or 10 balls. Using your palms or a rolling pin, flatten out each ball on a lightly floured board or plate until about 1 cm (½ inch) thick without tearing. Sprinkle with a little flour if the dough is too wet to work with.

Heat a little oil in a large frying pan over medium heat, add the flattened roti and cook until golden on both sides (make sure not to overcook or else it will be too hard). Remove from the pan and serve hot with coconut sambal.

Note *You can use plain (all-purpose) flour but self-raising flour will make the roti softer.*

Coconut roti
Pol roti

These are great served with tea country pork curry (see page 68).

MAKES 12

500 g (1 lb 2 oz) atta flour (see glossary)
50 g (1¾ oz) ghee (see glossary)
3 small green chillies, finely chopped
1 small onion, finely chopped
1 sprig curry leaves, leaves picked and finely chopped
1 cup freshly grated coconut (see glossary)
1 teaspoon salt
500 ml (17 fl oz/2 cups) warm water
100 ml (3½ fl oz) vegetable oil

Place the flour, ghee, chilli, onion, curry leaves, coconut and salt in a large bowl. Gradually add the water, a little at a time, using your hands to mix in and bring together to form smooth dough. Divide the dough into 12 balls, place in a bowl and set aside until ready to fry.

Take a ball of dough and, using your fingers, spread it out to form a thin disc, about 5 mm (¼ inch) thick and 10 cm (4 inches) in diameter.

Heat a small amount of the oil in a frying pan over high heat, add the roti and cook until it is loose enough to come off the pan, then flip and cook the other side until lightly crisped. Remove from the pan and set aside. Repeat with the remaining dough. Serve hot or at room temperature.

EGGPLANT ROTI TRIANGLES
BRINJAL ROTI

IN SRI LANKA, YOU SEE VENDORS MAKING THESE FRESH IN THE MORNING, FORMING THEM INTO PERFECT TRIANGLES THEN SEALING THEM ON THE HOTPLATE. IT'S GREAT WATCHING THEM COOK THESE, THEN EATING THEM FRESH OFF THE GRILL. A WORD OF CAUTION THOUGH, AS THESE ARE A LOCAL SNACK THEY ARE EXTREMELY SPICY.

MAKES 10

300 g (10 ½ oz/2 cups) plain (all-purpose) flour
2 tablespoons butter
½ teaspoon salt
250 ml (8 ½ fl oz/1 cup) water, or enough to make
   a moist but not sticky dough
100 ml (3 ½ fl oz) vegetable oil

EGGPLANT PICKLE
1 large eggplant (aubergine), cut into batons
1 small red onion quartered
2 green chillies, chopped
1 tablespoon ground turmeric, plus extra ½ teaspoon
500 ml (17 fl oz/2 cups) vegetable oil
2 sprigs curry leaves, leaves picked
4 garlic cloves, chopped
1 teaspoon black mustard seeds
½ teaspoon cumin seeds
1 tablespoon white sugar
1 tablespoon malt vinegar

Place the flour, butter and salt in a large bowl. Gradually add the water, a little at a time, using your hands to mix in and bring together to form a moist but not sticky ball of dough. Divide the dough into 10 balls, place in separate bowls, divide the oil among the bowls and leave to rest for 15 minutes.

Meanwhile, to make the eggplant pickle, place the eggplant, onion, chilli and 1 tablespoon of the turmeric in a bowl. Cover and shake to coat the eggplant.

Heat the oil in a wok or deep-sided saucepan to just below smoking point, add the eggplant mixture and cook until golden brown. Remove with a slotted spoon and drain on paper towel, then place in a bowl.

Heat 1 tablespoon of the frying oil in a small frying pan over medium heat, add the curry leaves, garlic, mustard seeds, cumin seeds, the extra ½ teaspoon of turmeric, the sugar and vinegar and cook until fragrant. Taste to check there is a balance of sweet and sour. Add to the eggplant mixture and gently mix.

Take a ball of dough and, using your fingers, spread it out to form a thin disc, about 5 mm (¼ inch) thick and 10 cm (4 inches) in diameter. Place 2 tablespoonfuls of the eggplant pickle in the centre. Fold the dough over the pickle and form into a triangle shape. Repeat with the remaining dough and pickle.

Heat some oil on a barbecue hotplate or in a large frying pan over low heat, place the roti on the hotplate and cook each side for about 3 minutes or until crisp. Serve hot.

Mrs Amarasakara's Hoppers

MAKING THESE IS AN ART AND TAKES SOME PRACTICE TO MASTER, BUT ONCE YOU'VE GOT IT DOWN PAT, YOU'LL HAVE AN ENDLESS SUPPLY OF FRIENDS WANTING TO COME AROUND FOR DINNER TO ENJOY THESE. I HATE TO SUGGEST THIS, BUT IF YOU'RE NOT PREPARED TO GO THROUGH THE WHOLE PROCESS OF MAKING THESE HOPPERS IN THE TRADITIONAL WAY, YOU CAN ALWAYS BUY A PACKET MIX — IT DOES WORK AND TASTES SIMILAR, BUT I ALWAYS FEEL THAT IT DOES NOT HAVE THE CRISP TEXTURE THAT THE FRESH COCONUT BRINGS TO THE HOPPER. THIS RECIPE INVOLVES SOME TRIAL AND ERROR ON YOUR PART (READ THE NOTES). FOR THIS RECIPE, YOU WILL NEED AT LEAST ONE HOPPER PAN (WITH A LID). HOPPER PANS ARE USUALLY MADE FROM ALUMINIUM AND AVAILABLE FROM SRI LANKAN OR INDIAN SUPERMARKETS — IT IS BEST TO KEEP THEM SOLELY FOR THE PURPOSES OF MAKING HOPPERS.

MAKES 10

1 fresh coconut
7 g (¼ oz) dried active yeast
100 ml (3½ fl oz) lukewarm milk (see notes)
1 teaspoon white sugar
2 cm (¾ inch) thick slice sourdough bread, broken up into pieces
500 g (1 lb 2 oz) rice flour
vegetable oil, for cooking
salt, to taste

Crack the coconut with the back of a large cleaver. Reserve the coconut water as it drains out for making the hoppers. Scrape out the white flesh and trim off the brown membrane. Grate the flesh with a hand-grater or in a food processor.

To make the first-extract coconut milk, place the grated flesh and 200 ml (7 fl oz) of water in a blender and, using the pulse action, process until everything is well combined and the flesh is soft. Line a sieve with muslin (cheesecloth) and place over a bowl. Pour in the blended coconut, then gather the sides of the muslin and squeeze to extract as much liquid as possible from the flesh. This is known as first-extract coconut milk or coconut cream. You should have 200 ml (7 fl oz) coconut cream. Set aside.

To make the second-extract coconut milk, repeat the process using the same coconut flesh, using 600 ml (20 fl oz) of water. You should have 400 ml (13½ fl oz) of coconut milk. Set aside and discard the coconut flesh.

Place the yeast, milk and sugar in a bowl, stir to combine and leave in a warm place for the yeast to activate — it should double in size and become frothy.

Combine the bread, reserved coconut water and second-extract coconut milk in a large bowl and whisk in the rice flour until it forms a thick batter.

Add the yeast mixture and whisk to combine. Set aside in a warm place for 6 hours to prove or until the mixture has doubled in size.

continued next page

continued from previous page

When the batter is ready, gently heat the first-extract coconut milk until lukewarm and set aside. Lightly grease the inside of a hopper pan with oil and place over high heat.

While the pan is heating, add the lukewarm first-extract coconut milk and stir to form a thick pancake-style batter. Season with salt.

Once the hopper pan is hot, working very quickly, add a ladleful of the batter and swirl to thinly coat the walls of the pan (see notes), making sure a small pool of batter remains at the bottom.

Cover pan with the lid and cook for 2–3 minutes or until the centre is firm and the sides are golden and crisp (see notes).

Lightly tap the sides of the pan to loosen the hopper (see notes), scoop out and serve hot.

Notes *It is very important that all of the liquids you use in this recipe are lukewarm. What that means is the liquid should not feel either cold or warm to the touch of the hand.*

If the hoppers are not thin enough, add a little more lukewarm water.

If the batter does not coat the pan when swirling the pan, the pan is too hot — reduce the heat.

If the edges of the hopper are not crispy, add another teaspoon of sugar to the batter.

If the hoppers are difficult to remove from the pan, add a beaten egg to the batter and stir well.

***Egg hoppers** are a a more substantial hopper and are popular all over Sri Lanka. Just before you cover the hopper pan with the lid, crack an egg into the hopper, cover and reduce the heat to medium. Cook for 3–5 minutes or until the edges of the hopper are crispy, the eggwhite is cooked and the yolk still soft. Remove from the pan as directed.*

STRING HOPPERS

STRING HOPPERS ARE STEAMED RICE NOODLE PANCAKES. THEY ARE MADE FROM A HOT-WATER DOUGH OF RICE FLOUR OR WHEAT FLOUR PRESSED OUT IN CIRCLETS FROM A STRING HOPPER MOULD (EITHER ALUMINIUM OR WOODEN) ONTO LITTLE WICKER MATS, THEN STEAMED. LIGHT AND LACY, STRING HOPPERS MAKE A MOUTH-WATERING MEAL WITH CURRY AND SAMBAL. STRING HOPPER MOULDS AND MATS ARE AVAILABLE FROM SRI LANKAN GROCERS.

MAKES 30 (PICTURED PAGE 207)

1 litre (34 fl oz/4 cups) water
450 g (1 lb) steamed wheat flour or rice flour (see note)
salt, to taste
coconut milk gravy (see page 193), to serve
coconut sambal (see page 176), to serve

Bring the water to the boil, pour it into a large bowl and cool slightly.

Pour in the flour, season with salt and stir to make a soft pliable dough, a bit softer than playdough.

Place the dough in a string hopper mould, squeeze out the dough onto a wicker mat and make an even double layer. Repeat squeezing out the remaining dough onto separate mats. Stack the mats on top of each other and steam for 3–5 minutes.

Serve with the coconut milk gravy and coconut sambal.

Note *My choice is wheat flour but for this recipe you have to steam the flour first. Wrap the wheat flour in a clean cloth and steam it for 1 hour in a bamboo steamer. While still hot, blend it to break it up and then sieve it. Alternatively, you can buy wheat flour steamed, ground and strained.*

You can also use rice flour, which doesn't require steaming, but it makes a different shape. You can buy white or red rice flour from Sri Lankan grocers.

From left to right: coconut sambal (see page 176),
coconut milk gravy (see page 193),
and string hoppers (see page 205).

NAAN BREAD

MAKES 8

100 ml (3 ½ fl oz) lukewarm milk
50 ml (1 ¾ fl oz) lukewarm water
7 g (⅙ oz) dried active yeast
1 teaspoon white sugar
100 g (3 ½ oz) plain yoghurt
80 g (3 oz) ghee (see glossary), melted and
   slightly cooled
750 g (1 lb 8 oz/5 cups) plain (all-purpose) flour
1 teaspoon salt
vegetable oil, for kneading and greasing

TOPPINGS (OPTIONAL)
50 g (1 ¾ oz) butter, melted
1 teaspoon nigella seeds
1 tablespoon minced garlic
1 tablespoon finely chopped coriander (cilantro)

Place the milk, water, sugar and yeast in a bowl and set aside for 5-10 minutes or until frothy.

Add the yoghurt and melted ghee and stir through.

Sift the flour and salt into a large bowl and make a well in the centre. Pour the yeast mixture into it. Using your hands, bring together to form a dough and knead firmly, turning it in on itself for 6-10 minutes or until the mixture comes away from the side of the bowl and the dough is soft and elastic. Add more water or flour during kneading if necessary.

Place the dough in a greased bowl, cover with a damp cloth and set aside for 3-4 hours to prove until doubled in size.

Remove the cloth, punch the mixture down, then knead for 2-3 minutes. Divide into 8 balls, place on a slightly oiled baking tray, cover with the damp cloth and set aside for 15 minutes to rest.

Preheat the oven to 260°C (500°F/Gas 9) or a barbecue with a hood to high. Place a pizza stone or heavy-based baking tray in the oven or on the barbecue to preheat.

Roll out each ball into a teardrop shape, ensuring they are quite thin and evenly rolled out.

You can leave the naan plain or brush the tops with the melted butter and sprinkle over a few nigella seeds, or brush with the garlic and sprinkle over the coriander.

Place on the pizza stone or tray and bake for 5-7 minutes or until the bread puffs and brown spots appear on it. Remove from the oven and wrap in a cloth to keep warm until serving.

CHAPATIS
MAKES 12

350 g (12 oz) atta flour (see glossary)
2 tablespoons ghee (see glossary), plus 2 tablespoons
    extra for greasing
150 ml (5 fl oz) water

Place the flour in a bowl. Add the water, a little at a time, mixing it all the time using your hand. Do not add too much water or it will be impossible to roll out.

Add the ghee and mix in — this will prevent the dough sticking to your hands during kneading. Knead until a nice dough (not too hard, not too soft) forms.

Divide the dough into balls, about 5 cm (2 inches) in diameter. Dust each ball with flour and shape into a 10 cm (4 inch) round. Dust again and then roll to about a 15 cm (6 inch) round.

Heat a tawa or large heavy-based frying pan over medium heat and lightly grease. Add the chapati, then turn after about 10 seconds. Turn again to cook the other side for 15–20 seconds. The chapati must not be turned more than three times, or the they will become like biscuits.

MALU PAAN

I CALL THESE ROLLS 'FISHERMAN'S DELIGHT'. WHENEVER I GO TO THE FISH MARKETS IN SRI LANKA THIS IS WHAT I EAT. IT SEEMS THAT THESE LITTLE SPICY BUNS ARE THE FIRST TO COME OUT OF THE SMALL BAKERIES AND ROADSIDE BOUTIQUES. THE BUN HAS TO BE SOFT AND THE MIXTURE INSIDE WARM.

MAKES 16

750 g (1 lb 10 oz/5 cups) baker's (strong) flour
60 g (2 oz) suet (available from the butcher), finely chopped
2 tablespoons caster (superfine) sugar
1 egg, lightly beaten
10 g (⅜ oz) dried active yeast
600 ml (20 fl oz) warm milk
2 teaspoons salt
1 egg yolk, for glazing
1 quantity egg rolls tuna filling (see page 30)

Place the flour in a bowl, rub in the suet until the mixture resembles coarse breadcrumbs, then add the sugar, beaten egg and yeast and combine well.

Gradually add the milk and mix until the dough comes together. Turn out onto a lightly floured work surface and knead for 3 minutes or until smooth and elastic.

Place the dough in a lightly oiled bowl, turn to coat, cover with a damp cloth and set aside in a warm place for 1 hour or until doubled in size.

Meanwhile, divide the filling into 16 pieces, shape into balls, place on a baking tray lined with baking paper and refrigerate until needed.

Preheat the oven to 200°C (390°F/Gas 6).

Punch down the dough, then divide into 16 balls. Working with one piece of dough at a time, flatten into a triangular shape about 1 cm thick. Place a ball of filling in the middle and fold the edges to form triangular-shaped rolls.

Place the parcels on a baking tray lined with baking paper, brush all over with the beaten egg yolk and bake for 7–10 minutes or until the glaze starts to brown. The rolls have to be soft so don't overcook them. If not eating immediately, cool the rolls and freeze straight away.

CRUSTY BREAD

GROWING UP IN COLOMBO, WE LIVED NEXT DOOR TO THE VILLAGE BAKERY. I WAS A FRIEND OF THE BAKER'S SON AND OUR PLAYGROUND WAS THE STORE ROOM FILLED WITH FLOUR SACKS BEHIND THE LARGE, VERY OLD, WOOD-FIRED OVEN. THIS IS THE TYPE OF BREAD YOU WILL FIND EVERYWHERE IN SRI LANKA — IT'S LIGHT AND CRUSTY AND IS THE PERFECT BREAD TO HAVE WARM WITH COCONUT SAMBAL (SEE PAGE 176).

MAKES 2 LOAVES / 12 ROLLS

450 g (1 lb) baker's (strong) flour
1 teaspoon salt
80 g (2¾ oz) margarine
15 g (½ oz) dried active yeast
2 teaspoons caster (superfine) sugar
250 ml (8½ fl oz/1 cup) warm milk
75 ml (2½ fl oz) warm water
coconut oil, for brushing

Place the flour and salt in a large bowl, then rub the margarine into the flour.

Combine the yeast, sugar, milk and water in a bowl, then add to the flour mixture and combine until a soft but dry dough forms — you may need to add a little more flour if the mixture is too wet.

Turn the dough out onto a lightly floured work surface and knead for 5–7 minutes or until smooth and elastic. Place the dough in a lightly oiled bowl, turn to coat, then cover with a damp cloth and set aside in a warm place for 1 hour or until doubled in size.

Preheat the oven to 200°C (390°F/Gas 6).

Punch the dough down and shape into two loaves or 12 rolls. Place on a heavy-based baking tray, brush with the coconut oil and bake for 35–40 minutes or until golden and the bases sound hollow when tapped.

JAFFNA UPPUMA

THIS IS AN ALTERNATIVE TO RICE.
AS A RULE, JAFFNA UPPUMA REQUIRES
TWO MEASURES OF WATER FOR EACH
MEASURE OF SEMOLINA.

SERVES 4

180 g (6 oz/1 cup) semolina
50 ml (1¾ fl oz) vegetable oil
½ teaspoon black mustard seeds
1 sprig curry leaves, leaves picked
¼ teaspoon ground turmeric
1 onion, diced
1 garlic clove, minced
2 dried red chillies, broken into pieces
500 ml (17 fl oz/2 cups) water
salt, to taste
1 spring onion (scallion) (white part only), thinly sliced
1 long red chilli, seeds removed and thinly sliced

In a dry frying pan over medium heat, lightly toast the semolina, shaking the pan occasionally. Set aside.

Heat the oil in a frying pan over high heat, add the mustard seeds and cook until they start to pop. Add the curry leaves, turmeric, onion, garlic and chilli pieces and cook until the onion is golden.

Reduce the heat to low, add the toasted semolina and water, season with salt and stir constantly to avoid lumps until the mixture is well cooked, about 8 minutes. Garnish with the spring onion and chilli to serve.

Variation *You can add vegetables, such as carrots, green beans or cauliflower. Cut the vegetables into small pieces and steam, then add to the pan along with the onion before adding the semolina.*

BREADFRUIT CHIPS

WHEN I WAS WORKING IN FIJI, MY STAFF USED TO CALL THE CANAPÉS AT THE BEGINNING OF A MEAL 'PICKIES'. ONE OF THE PICKIES WE HAD ON THE MENU WERE THESE BREADFRUIT CHIPS — THEY TASTE SO GOOD AND HAVE A LOVELY CRUNCH TO THEM.

SERVES 5

300 ml (10 fl oz) vegetable oil
1 breadfruit (see glossary), peeled and thinly sliced
½ teaspoon salt
½ teaspoon ground black pepper
½ teaspoon red chilli powder

Heat the oil in a saucepan over high heat until it reaches smoking point. Add the breadfruit and deep-fry, stirring occasionally, until crisp and golden. Remove with a slotted spoon and drain on paper towel.

Place the salt, pepper and chilli powder in a bowl and toss the breadfruit chips in the mixture to coat.

CASSAVA RICE

CASSAVA IS AVAILABLE FROZEN BUT YOU MAY BE LUCKY AND FIND IT FRESH IN ASIAN VEGETABLE MARKETS. SERVE WITH GRILLED FISH AND SALAD, SUCH AS THE GRILLED YELLOWTAIL (SEE PAGE 139).

SERVES 6 AS A SIDE

200 g (7 oz) cassava flour (see note)
100 g (3½ oz) freshly grated coconut
1 teaspoon salt

Sift the cassava flour into a saucepan, then add the coconut and stir constantly over medium heat, with no oil, until the cassava and coconut form a rice-like starch. Serve in a communal bowl.

Note *It is preferable to make your own flour from fresh or frozen cassava, which is dried in the sun or in a very low oven and then grated.*

GRILLED BANANA

UTENSILS ARE NOT ALWAYS AVAILABLE ON THE ISLANDS AND COOKING ON AN OPEN FIRE CAN ADD UNWANTED FOREIGN MATTER TO YOUR FOOD. THROWING THE BANANAS ON WHOLE KEEPS THE INSIDES MOIST AND GIVES THE BANANAS A BEAUTIFUL SMOKY FLAVOUR. THE BANANAS MUST BE OF THE COOKING VARIETY SO THEY END UP SOFT AND TASTY. SERVE WITH SEAFOOD CAKES (SEE PAGE 132).

2 cooking bananas per person, unpeeled

Place bananas in the coals of a fire or on a hot barbecue grill plate. Cook, turning occasionally, until blackened all over and a knife slides through them easily. Remove from the fire and cool for 5 minutes before removing the peel and eating.

ROASTED BREADFRUIT

THIS STARCHY FRUIT HAS A BREAD-LIKE TEXTURE AND A SWEET TASTE BUT IS USED LIKE A VEGETABLE. IT MAY BE DIFFICULT TO LOCATE, BUT YOU MIGHT FIND IT AT ASIAN FRUIT AND VEGETABLE MARKETS. SERVE WITH SEAFOOD CAKES (SEE PAGE 132).

SERVES 2

1 small breadfruit

Place the whole breadfruit in the coals of a fire or on a large gas flame on the stove. Cook, turning occasionally, until blackened all over and a knife slides through it easily. Remove from the fire and cool for 5 minutes. Carefully slice off the skin to reveal the soft centre.

FOOLPROOF STEAMED RICE

EVEN THOUGH MOST PEOPLE USE RICE COOKERS NOWADAYS IT IS GOOD TO KNOW A FOOLPROOF WAY OF COOKING RICE WITHOUT ONE. I HAVE FOUND THAT THE DISTANCE BETWEEN THE FIRST JOINT AND THE END OF A FINGER IS RELATIVELY THE SAME FOR MOST ADULTS. THIS FIRST JOINT IS YOUR VERY PORTABLE WATER GAUGE. YOU CAN USE THIS METHOD TO MAKE AS MUCH RICE AS YOU NEED. I USUALLY WORK ON 1 CUP OF UNCOOKED RICE PER PERSON.

SERVES 4

5 cups any type of rice
salt, to taste

Take the amount of raw rice you require and wash it thoroughly in cool water only once. Rice is so highly polished these days that if you wash it any more you will wash away the goodness. If you are cooking this in Asia, then it may need washing two or three times depending on where you bought the rice and how well it has been husked. You may also have to remove any stones or other foreign matter that has found its way into your rice.

Now flatten the washed rice in the base of a large saucepan and add enough water until it reaches from the top of the rice to the first joint of your middle finger. For brown rice, add a little more.

Add salt and bring to the boil over high heat, uncovered, and continue to cook until you can see the top of the rice and the water has evaporated to that level.

Reduce the heat to as low as possible (if your stovetop is electric, have the hotplate next to it on the lowest setting ready to go, and transfer it across), cover with a lid and leave to steam for about 10 minutes. Do not stir or open the lid as you don't want to loose any steam so the rice so will be fluffy and dry.

Once ready, remove the lid and, using the handle of a wooden spoon, fluff the rice. Cover until ready to serve.

ரியோ ஐஸ்-கிரீம் **Rio** *Ice Cream*
 රියෝ අයිස්ක්‍රීම්

RIO ICE CREAM

Sweets

HALO HALO

I WAS LUCKY ENOUGH TO PREPARE THIS DISH IN AN AMAZING PLACE CALLED THE CHOCOLATE HILLS IN THE PHILIPPINES. THE AREA HAS THESE HUGE GRASS-COVERED LIMESTONE MOUNDS FOR AS FAR AS THE EYE CAN SEE. THEY HAVE BEEN GIVEN THIS TITLE BECAUSE IN SUMMER THE GRASS THAT COVERS THEM TURNS BROWN AND THE WHOLE REGION LOOKS LIKE A SEA OF CHOCOLATE HILLS. LEGEND HAS IT THAT THE HILLS WERE FORMED FROM THE TEARS OF A HEARTBROKEN GIANT. YOU CAN EAT HALO HALO AS IS OR MIX THE WHOLE CONCOCTION BEFORE EATING. SOME OF THE INGREDIENTS, SUCH AS THE CORN OR FRUITS, MAY BE REPLACED WITH CHERRIES, CRUSHED PINEAPPLE, PAPAYA OR ANY OTHER RIPE FRUITS IN SEASON.

SERVES 4

½ cup drained tinned corn kernels or cooked chickpeas
1 cup cooked sweet potato (yam) or glutinous purple yam (ube halaya), cut into 2.5 cm (1 inch) cubes
1 cup drained tinned ripe jackfruit (see glossary), thinly sliced
2 ripe mangoes, peeled (or 1 cup tinned mango), cut into 1 cm (½ inch) pieces
1 large ripe banana, sliced
1 cup fresh or drained tinned young shredded coconut
1 cup cubed jelly (see note)
2 cups shaved ice
250 ml (8½ fl oz/1 cup) evaporated milk
4 scoops of your favourite ice cream
wafer, chopped peanuts or crisped rice cereal, to serve (optional)

Divide the corn, sweet potato, jackfruit, mango, banana, coconut and jelly between four tall serving glasses. Top each glass with ½ cup of the shaved ice, 60 ml (2 fl oz/ 3 tablespoons) of the milk and a scoop of ice cream. Serve with a wafer or sprinkle over the nuts or cereal (if using), and serve immediately.

Note *To make the jelly, soak 1½ sheets titanium-strength gelatine in iced water. Heat 1 cup fruit juice in a saucepan over low heat. When the gelatine is soft, drain and squeeze out the excess water. Add to the pan and stir until dissolved. Do not boil. Remove from the heat and pour into a small tray, refrigerate until set, then cut into 1 cm (½ inch) cubes.*

From left to right: earl grey chocolate truffles (see page 226), and coffee and pandan flan (see page 227).

EARL GREY CHOCOLATE TRUFFLES

I CREATED THESE FOR THE DILMAH FAMILY WHILE FILMING *MY SRI LANKA*. CACAO TREES ARE COMMERCIALLY GROWN ON THE ISLAND AND CHOCOLATE MAKES A WONDERFUL PAIRING WITH THE BERGAMOT IN EARL GREY TEA.

MAKES ABOUT 25 (PICTURED PAGE 224)

160 ml (5¼ fl oz) thick (double) cream
40 g (1½ oz) unsalted butter, cut into 4 pieces
  and softened
2 teaspoons earl grey tea leaves
175 g (6 oz) good-quality bittersweet chocolate
  (not unsweetened), chopped

Bring the cream and butter to the boil in a small heavy-based saucepan, then stir in the tea leaves, remove from the heat and leave for 5 minutes to infuse.

Meanwhile, finely grind the chocolate in a food processor, then transfer to a bowl. Strain the cream mixture through a fine mesh sieve onto the chocolate, pressing on the leaves, then whisk until smooth. Discard the tea leaves. Cover and refrigerate for about 2 hours or until firm.

Roll into walnut-sized balls. Leave at room temperature to serve. Store leftovers in an airtight container in the refrigerator but bring to room temperature before serving.

Coffee and pandan flan

I was inspired to make this dish after being invited in Sulawesi, Indonesia, to harvest the seaweed that is used to make agar agar. I always smile to myself when I think about these very simple ingredients making their way into the kitchens of some of the best chefs in the world. Agar Agar has been used by Asians for centuries and is now sold at exorbitant prices in specialty stores as part of spherification kits for molecular gastronomy. The people who harvest this commodity would be astonishedto know how far their product travels.

MAKES 6 (PICTURED PAGE 225)

sliced mango, whipped cream and grated palm sugar (jaggery), to serve

BASE
2 teaspoons agar agar powder
875 ml (30 fl oz/3½ cups) good-quality plunger-brewed coffee, double-strained
100 g (3½ oz/¾ cup) grated palm sugar (jaggery)
2 teaspoons vanilla essence or seeds from ½ vanilla bean

TOP
2 teaspoons agar agar powder
875 ml (30 fl oz/3½ cups) coconut milk
100 g (3½ oz/¾ cup) grated palm sugar (jaggery)
2 cm (¾ inch) piece of pandan leaf (see glossary)
1 teaspoon vanilla essence or ½ vanilla bean, split and seeds scraped
½ teaspoon salt

To make the base, place all of the ingredients in a saucepan over low heat, stirring until the sugar dissolves, and bring to the boil. Remove from the heat and divide among six 200 ml (7 fl oz) capacity glasses. Cool, then refrigerate for 1 hour or until set.

When the bases have set, make the top. Place the agar agar, coconut milk and palm sugar in a saucepan over low heat and stir until the sugar dissolves. Add the pandan leaf and bring to the boil, then add the vanilla and salt and combine well.

Remove from the heat and leave to cool, then remove and discard the pandan leaf. Pour the mixture over the top of the bases and refrigerate for another 2 hours or until set.

Garnish with the mango, cream and sugar to serve.

Note *If you wish to serve the flan unmoulded, make the top first, then cover with the base. Turn the flan out of the mould like you would jelly.*

SAGO PUDDING WITH MACE

INDONESIA IS FAMOUS FOR ITS SPICES, AND NUTMEG AND MACE ARE THE JEWELS IN ITS CROWN. MACE IS THE OUTER SKIN OF THE NUTMEG SEED, SURROUNDING THAT IS THE FLESH, WHICH IS CANDIED AND USED IN DESSERTS.

WHILE WE WERE FILMING THE SORTING PROCESS IN THE BANDA ISLANDS I WAS SITTING ON A LARGE SET OF SCALES WATCHING THE BOYS WORK INSIDE A VERY HOT HOUSE. ALL OF A SUDDEN THE SCALES STARTED TO SHAKE VIOLENTLY, AND THE BOYS JUST DISAPPEARED. THERE WAS ALSO A LARGE AUDIENCE OF KIDS PEERING THROUGH EVERY OPENING IN THE BUILDING WHO DISAPPEARED TOO. THE REASON FOR THE EXODUS WAS THAT A LARGE EARTHQUAKE WAS ON THE WAY AND THE LOCALS HAD A SIXTH SENSE ABOUT IT. TWO WEEKS AFTER WE LEFT THE ISLAND, ITS LIVE VOLCANO BLEW ITS TOP, SPEWING ROCK, ASH AND LAVA TWO KILOMETRES INTO THE SKY. WE WERE LUCKY TO ESCAPE SUCH A CLOSE CALL.

SERVES 6

300 g (10 ½ oz) sago
1 litre (34 fl oz/4 cups) water
pinch of ground cinnamon
3 pieces fresh or dried mace, plus extra to serve
30 g (1 oz) grated dark palm sugar (jaggery)
100 g (3 ½ oz) white sugar
1 litre (34 fl oz/4 cups) coconut cream

Place the sago and water in a saucepan over medium heat and cook, stirring occasionally, until it comes to the boil.

When it starts to thicken, add the cinnamon, mace, sugars and all but 2 tablespoons of the coconut cream. Reduce the heat to low and cook, stirring constantly (or the mixture will stick to the base of the pan), for 8–10 minutes or until the sago is translucent.

Remove from the heat and divide among bowls. Drizzle with the remaining coconut cream and scatter with the extra mace. Serve immediately.

BANANA POKE WITH COCONUT SORBET

THE FIRST TIME I TASTED THIS DISH WAS IN THE COOK ISLANDS. PRONOUNCED 'PO' AS IN PORK AND 'KE' AS IN KETTLE, BANANA POKE REALLY IS A HEAVENLY DESSERT. ARROWROOT IS NOT WIDELY USED THESE DAYS BUT YOU CAN BUY IT FROM MOST ASIAN GROCERS. IF YOU ARE NOT A BANANA LOVER, TRY THIS DISH WITH PINEAPPLE OR MANGO.

MAKES 12

250 g (9 oz) peeled overripe bananas
150 g (5 oz) palm sugar
1 litre (34 fl oz/4 cups) water
375 g (13 oz) arrowroot starch
½ teaspoon vanilla essence
juice of ½ lime
fresh tropical fruit, to serve (optional)

COCONUT SORBET
500 ml (17 fl oz/2 cups) water
350 g (12 oz) white sugar
400 ml (13 fl oz) coconut milk

To make the coconut sorbet, bring the water and sugar to the boil. Allow to cool, then mix in the coconut milk. Churn in an ice-cream machine according to the manufacturer's instructions, then freeze until serving.

To make the banana poke, preheat the oven to 170°C (340°F/Gas 3) and lightly grease a 12-hole muffin tray.

Place the bananas, palm sugar and water into a heavy-based saucepan. Bring to the boil over high heat, then reduce to a simmer.

Cook for about 30 minutes or until the bananas turn a purple colour. Set aside in the liquid to cool and then strain.

Mash the cooled banana and mix in the arrowroot, vanilla and lime juice. The mixture should not be sticky. If it is, add a little more arrowroot.

Spoon the mixture into the greased muffin tray and bake for 30–45 minutes, or until a skewer inserted into the centre comes out clean.

Turn the poke out onto a wire rack to cool. Serve warm or cold with the coconut sorbet and topped with fresh tropical fruit, if desired.

JAFFNA BANANA SPLIT

I ARRIVED IN JAFFNA IN SRI LANKA JUST AFTER THE END OF THE CIVIL WAR, THINGS WERE STILL TENSE THERE AND WE WERE THE FIRST FILM CREW ALLOWED TO ENTER THE REGION AND FILM IN THE PAST THIRTY YEARS. DURING OUR TRAVELS AROUND THIS VIBRANT CITY WE CAME ACROSS A BEAUTIFUL DUTCH CHURCH, WHICH WAS A WORKING MONASTERY OF FRANCISCAN FRIARS. THEY WERE A FRIENDLY LOT WHO COULD PLAY CRICKET LIKE DEMONS. THEY ALSO MADE A VERY NICE SWEET WINE. ANOTHER UNIQUE FEATURE OF JAFFNA IS THE FIFTIES-STYLE ICE-CREAM PARLOURS, SO IT SEEMED ONLY NATURAL TO RECREATE MY FAVOURITE CHILDHOOD DESSERT FOR THE SHOW. I MADE THIS BANANA SPLIT, GIVING IT A GROWN-UP MAKEOVER USING THE FRIARS' SWEET WINE AS A SYRUP.

SERVES 6

100 g (3½ oz) jackfruit (see glossary), peeled and diced
6 sugar bananas, peeled and halved lengthways
2 oranges, peeled, pith removed and segmented
6 scoops vanilla ice cream
200 ml (7 fl oz) thin (pouring) cream, whipped

MULLED WINE REDUCTION
750 ml (25 fl oz/3 cups) fortified wine, such as port or tokay
1 cinnamon stick, broken up
220 g (8 oz/1 cup) white sugar
8 whole cloves
1 piece of mace
peel of 1 orange, white pith removed
peel of 1 lime, white pith removed

TOFFEE PEANUTS
150 g (5 oz) raw peanuts, plus extra to garnish
vegetable oil, for greasing
100 g (3½ oz) white sugar
80 ml (3 fl oz/⅓ cup) water

To make the mulled wine reduction, place all of the ingredients in a saucepan over medium heat and cook for 10 minutes or until the mixture is quite sticky and significantly reduced. Remove from the heat and set aside until ready to serve. Strain before using, discarding the solids.

To make the toffee peanuts, place the peanuts in a small saucepan over low heat. Stir constantly for a few minutes or until the peanuts have started to brown. Remove immediately from the heat and spread on a plate to stop them from cooking further.

Lightly brush a baking tray with oil and set aside. Wipe the pan used to toast the peanuts and return to medium–high heat. Add the sugar and water, stirring once to combine, then leave to cook, without stirring, for 10 minutes or until the toffee is golden and caramelised, with an even colour. If the toffee starts to stick to the sides of the pan, use a wet pastry brush to wipe it off.

Once it is golden, immediately remove from the heat, quickly add the peanuts and stir to combine. Quickly but carefully pour the toffee peanuts onto the prepared tray and spread out. Leave to completely cool before breaking into shards.

To serve, cover the base of each plate with the wine reduction, divide the jackfruit, banana and orange among the plates, and top with some ice cream, a dollop of whipped cream, the toffee peanut shards and extra peanuts.

TIM'S BANANA BREAD

THIS RECIPE IS ONE OF THE BEST I'VE TASTED. ONE OF MY CHEFS AT FLYING FISH CREATED IT. I HAVE LOVED EATING BANANAS SINCE I WAS VERY YOUNG AND MY AUNTY NANDAS ALWAYS HAD A LARGE HAND OF BANANAS WAITING FOR ME WHEN I VISITED HER.

SERVES 8–10

500 g (1 lb 2 oz) ripe bananas, mashed
450 g (1 lb) caster (superfine) sugar
4 eggs, at room temperature
115 ml (3 ¾ fl oz) vegetable oil
450 g (1 lb) plain (all-purpose) flour
25 g (⅞ oz) baking powder
150 g (5 oz) butter, melted and slightly cooled

RUM SYRUP
100 ml (3 ½ fl oz) rum
80 g (2 ¾ oz) caster (superfine) sugar

Preheat the oven to 160°C (320°F/Gas 2–3). Lightly grease a 30 x 12 cm (12 x 4½ inch) loaf (bar) tin and line with baking paper.

Beat the banana and sugar together in a large bowl.

Beat the eggs and oil together in another bowl and add to the banana purée.

Sift the flour and baking powder together and gently fold into the banana mixture. Gradually add the melted butter and fold in. Pour into the prepared tin.

Bake for 50–70 minutes or until a skewer inserted into the centre comes out clean.

Meanwhile, to make the rum syrup, warm the rum slightly in a saucepan, add the sugar and stir until dissolved.

Remove the cake from the oven and brush generously with the rum syrup. Leave to cool in the tin.

Slice into thick slabs and drizzle with any remaining syrup.

BREAD AND BUTTER PUDDING

THIS BRITISH CLASSIC HAS FOUND ITS WAY INTO THE HEARTS OF MANY SRI LANKANS. MY MUM TAUGHT ME HOW TO MAKE THIS. IT'S A GREAT WAY TO USE UP STALE BREAD.

SERVES 6

500 ml (17 fl oz/2 cups) milk
225 g (8 oz) stale bread, broken into small pieces
5 eggs, at room temperature
55 g (2 oz) unsalted butter or margarine
175 g (6 oz) white sugar
2 teaspoon vanilla essence
85 g (3 oz/½ cup) raisins (optional)
225 g (8 oz) sweet marmalade or jam

Preheat the oven to 200°C (390°F/Gas 6).

Bring the milk to the boil in a saucepan, then remove from the heat. Add the bread and leave to soak for 15 minutes.

Beat the eggs and sugar well in a bowl, then add the bread mixture, vanilla essence and raisins and mix well.

Coat the insides of a 30 x 15 cm (12 x 6 inch), 1 litre (34 fl oz/4 cup) capacity baking dish with the marmalade and add the pudding mixture. Cover with foil, place the dish in a roasting tray and add enough water to reach halfway up the sides of the baking dish. Bake for about 40 minutes or until the custard is set. Remove from oven and carefully invert onto a serving dish.

VANILLA CUSTARD WITH ALMOND SPONGE CRUMBLE

MAKES 6

RASPBERRY JELLY
125 g (4½ oz) caster (superfine) sugar
250 ml (8½ fl oz/1 cup) water
250 g (9 oz) raspberries
titanium-strength gelatine leaves (6–7 g/¼ oz each leaf)

VANILLA CUSTARD
60 ml (2 fl oz/3 tablespoons) milk
125 ml (4 fl oz/½ cup) thin (pouring) cream
½ vanilla bean, split and seeds scraped,
   plus thin slivers to garnish
2 egg yolks, at room temperature
30 g (1 oz) caster (superfine) sugar

ALMOND SPONGE
2 whole eggs, at room temperature
55 g (2 oz/¼ cup) caster (superfine) sugar
55 g (2 oz/¼ cup) ground almonds

PASSIONFRUIT CREAM
75 ml (2½ fl oz) passionfruit pulp
25 g (⅞ oz) caster (superfine) sugar
300 ml (10 fl oz) thin (pouring) cream
100 ml (3½ fl oz) thick (double) cream

To make the raspberry jelly, bring the sugar and water to the boil in a large saucepan, stirring to dissolve the sugar.

Place the raspberries in a heatproof bowl, pour over the sugar syrup and using a hand-held stick blender, blend until smooth. Strain into a large measuring jug, discarding the solids.

Using the ratio of 7 leaves of titanium-strength gelatine to 1 litre (34 fl oz/4 cups) of raspberry liquid, soak the correct amount of gelatine in cold water until softened.

Heat the measured amount of raspberry liquid in a small saucepan, squeeze the water from the gelatine and add to the pan, stirring until completely dissolved. Remove from the heat and divide among 185 ml (6 fl oz/¾ cup) capacity serving glasses. Refrigerate for 3–4 hours or until set.

To make the vanilla custard, place the milk, cream and vanilla seeds in a large saucepan over medium heat and bring just to the boil, then remove from the heat.

Beat the egg yolks and sugar together in a heatproof bowl until light and fluffy. Add the hot milk mixture, then return to the pan over low heat and cook, stirring constantly or until the mixture reaches 83°C (181°F) on a thermometer or coats the back of a wooden spoon.

Immediately remove from the heat and strain into a jug. Press plastic wrap onto the surface and refrigerate until needed.

To make the almond sponge, preheat the oven to 200°C (390°F/Gas 6). Lightly grease two baking trays and line with baking paper.

Beat the eggs using an electric mixer until very light and fluffy. Remove the bowl from the mixer and, using a rubber spatula, gently fold the ground almonds. Spread onto the prepared trays to 5 cm (2 inches) thick and bake for 8–10 minutes or until crumbly and golden.

Remove from the oven and leave to cool, then cut into rounds small enough to fit into your serving glasses. I suggest using the top of the glasses as the cutter.

To make the passionfruit cream, bring the passionfruit pulp and sugar to the boil in a small saucepan, stirring until the sugar is dissolved. Strain through a fine mesh sieve into a bowl, discarding the solids. Refrigerate until cool.

Place the creams in a large bowl and whisk just until soft peaks form. Gently fold in the passionfruit syrup. Refrigerate until needed.

To assemble, layer the vanilla custard, almond sponge and passionfruit cream over the jelly in the glasses and garnish each with a slither of vanilla bean.

GRAPEFRUIT AND CAMPARI SORBET

THIS IS COOL AND REFRESHING TO EAT WHILE ON THE HOT SRI LANKAN COAST. IT MAKES USE OF THE GRAPEFRUITS FOUND IN THE LOCAL MARKETS. IF POSSIBLE, FRESHLY SQUEEZE AND STRAIN YOUR OWN GRAPEFRUIT JUICE.

MAKES ABOUT 1.75 LITRES (4 PT)

750 ml (25 fl oz/3 cups) pink grapefruit juice
500 ml (17 fl oz/2 cups) simple sugar syrup (see note)
500 ml (17 fl oz/2 cups) water
60 ml (2 fl oz/3 tablespoons) Campari
25 ml (¾ fl oz) lime juice, strained

Combine all of the ingredients in a large bowl. Churn in an ice-cream machine according to the manufacturer's instructions, then freeze until serving.

Note *To make simple sugar syrup, combine 220 g (8 oz/1 cup) white sugar and 250 ml (8½ fl oz/1 cup) water in a saucepan over medium–high heat and stir until the sugar has dissolved. Bring to the boil, then remove from the heat and cool before using. Makes 500 ml (17 fl oz/2 cups).*

ROSEHIP AND HIBISCUS SORBET

TEA IS SUCH A GREAT WAY TO INFUSE SUBTLE FLAVOUR INTO DESSERTS. THIS WAS ONE OF THE ORIGINAL DISHES I CREATED FOR THE DILMAH FAMILY.

MAKES 1.5 LITRES (3 PT 3 FL OZ)

1.3 litres (2 pt 10 fl oz) water
50 g (1¾ oz) rosehip and hibiscus tea
500 ml (17 fl oz/2 cups) hibiscus syrup (see note)
juice of 2 limes, strained
hibiscus in syrup (see note), drained, to garnish

Bring the water to the boil, add the tea leaves and leave to cool. Strain into a bowl, discarding the solids.
  Mix in the syrup and lime juice. Churn in an ice-cream machine according to the manufacturer's instructions, then freeze until serving.

Note *Hibiscus in syrup is available from gourmet food stores.*

Rosehip and hibiscus sorbet

CHOCOLATE FONDANT PUDDING WITH MALTED CREAM

ONE OF MY FAVOURITES FROM A RESTAURANT IN FIJI, YOU CAN MAKE THE PUDDING MIX AHEAD OF TIME AND KEEP COOL UNTIL YOU'RE READY TO BAKE.

MAKES 10

CHOCOLATE FONDANT PUDDING

250 g (9 oz) unsalted butter, chopped
50 g (1¾ oz) cocoa powder, sifted
250 g (9 oz) dark chocolate, chopped
5 whole eggs, at room temperature
5 egg yolks, at room temperature
300 g (10½ oz) caster (superfine) sugar
250 g (9 oz/1⅔ cups) plain (all-purpose) flour, sifted

STRAWBERRY SYRUP

100 g (3½ oz) caster (superfine) sugar
50 ml (1¾ fl oz) water
250 g (9 oz) strawberries, hulled and halved

MALTED CREAM

75 g (2½ oz) chocolate malt powder
1 vanilla bean, split lengthways and seeds scraped
100 g (3½ oz) thick (double) cream
100 ml (3½ fl oz) thin (pouring) cream

To make the chocolate fondant puddings, preheat the oven to 160°C (320°F/Gas 2–3) and lightly spray ten 150 ml (5 fl oz) capacity dariole moulds with cooking oil.

Place the chocolate, butter and cocoa powder in a large heatproof bowl, place over a saucepan of simmering water and melt together until smooth and combined, stirring occasionally. Remove from the heat.

Whisk the whole eggs and egg yolks together in a large bowl. Gradually add the sugar and whisk until pale and creamy.

Add one-third of the chocolate mixture to the eggs and mix to combine, then gently fold in the remaining chocolate mixture.

Using a rubber spatula, carefully fold in the flour. Divide among the moulds and smooth the top with the back of a spoon and place on a baking tray.

Bake for 12–15 minutes or until cooked on the top and gooey in the middle. Do not overcook — the centre should still be runny. Remove from the oven and leave for a few minutes to set.

To make the strawberry syrup, bring the sugar and water to the boil in a saucepan, stirring until the sugar is dissolved. Add the strawberries, reduce the heat to low and cook for about 10 minutes or until most of the sugar syrup has evaporated. Remove from the heat and allow to cool.

To make the malted cream, place the malt powder, vanilla seeds and creams in a large bowl and whisk just until soft peaks form. Refrigerate until ready to serve.

To serve, gently ease each pudding from its mould and place on a plate. Spoon over the strawberry syrup and place a scoop of malted cream alongside. When the puddings are cut, the liquid chocolate should ooze out.

Glossary

ANNATTO OIL

Also called atsuete oil; simply vegetable oil coloured with annatto seeds. To make it, heat 80 ml (3 fl oz/⅓ cup) of vegetable oil and 1 teaspoon annatto seeds in a saucepan over low heat for a few minutes, being careful not to burn the seeds. Remove from the heat and allow to cool, then strain the oil. Makes 80 ml (3 fl oz/⅓ cup).

ANNATTO SEEDS

These small, red, pyramid-shaped seeds have a peppery taste and are used as a natural colouring in confectionary and other foods.

ASAFOETIDA

Also known as *hing*, this powdered gum resin imparts a very strong onion–garlic flavor to dishes and is what gives Indian curries their distinctive flavour. It's available from Indian grocers or health food stores.

ATTA FLOUR

A wholemeal flour made from ground wheat grains and commonly used in making Indian flat breads.

AYLESBURY DUCK

This type of duck is primarily bred for meat production. A similar variety that may be more widely available is the Pekin duck.

BANANA, FRUIT AND LEAVES

The banana fruit is also eaten, both ripe and green (unripe). Commonly used throughout Asia, the large pliable leaves are used to wrap foods for steaming or baking, such as in lap lap, the popular dish from Vanuatu. They help retain moisture and infuse a mild flavour into food.

BANANA BUD

This small part of the banana plant is harvested just after the banana fruit forms. It is usually treated as a vegetable and can be used in stews or salads.

BETEL LEAF

An edible vine leaf used to wrap food. It's popular in South-East Asian cuisines. You can buy betel leaves from Asian grocers.

BITTER GOURD

Also called bitter melon, *karavila* and *ampalaya*, this sour vegetable is widely used in salads, stir-fries and curries. It's highly valued for its medicinal properties.

BLACK MUSTARD SEEDS (ABA)

Always try to buy small black ones, can be used whole or finely ground. Try frying whole in oil with curry leaves and onion, or dry roasting.

BLACK PEPPERCORNS

Use whole black peppercorns when cooking Sri Lankan dishes; they are typically spicier than the white variety.

BOMBAY ONION

These are small red onions typically used in Sri Lankan and Indian cooking. You can substitute French shallots or red Asian shallots.

BREADFRUIT

This starchy fruit has a bread-like texture and a sweet taste but is used like a vegetable and can be boiled, roasted, fried, baked or barbecued.

CALAMANSI

These are a citrus fruit similar to lemons and are widely used in the Philippines. They can be substituted with lemons.

CANDIED NUTMEG

The candied fruit of the nutmeg tree; its flavour is similar to nutmeg spice (which is made from the seed of the same fruit) but is a little milder.

CANDLENUTS

These waxy nuts are usually ground to thicken Indonesian curries. They must be cooked before eating as they are highly toxic when raw.

CANE VINEGAR (SUKANG ILOKO)

This is made from sugarcane and is used in Filipino cooking to add a sour note.

CARDAMOM PODS

Whole or ground, cardamom is a fragrant spice often used in sweet dishes.

CASSAVA

The starchy root of the cassava plant is usually boiled and served as a staple accompaniment to dishes, much like rice.

CASSAVA FLOUR

This can be bought at shops but it is preferable to make your own flour from fresh or frozen cassava by drying it in the sun or in a very low oven, and then grating it.

CHILLI FLAKES

Suited to certain dishes more than chilli powder. Choosing chilli flakes without dust in the bottom of the bag is key.

CHILLI POWDER

Made from ground dried chillies. It's important to stick to one brand of chilli powder to be sure you're familiar with the intensity.

CHILLIES

There are many different types of chillies such as green chillies, bird's eye chillies and dried chillies. Green chillies are often hotter than red. Sri Lankan cuisine is typically fairly fiery but you should add chillies to suit your own tastes. Use fresh or dried for varying heat and flavour.

CINNAMON STICKS

A significant spice in Sri Lankan cooking, used in sweet and savoury dishes. Whole sticks ground for the meal at hand are far superior to pre-ground cinnamon.

CLAY CHATTY

A delicately glazed clay pot used on wood fires, it can also be used for cooking on a gas stove. Various shapes and sizes of clay chatties are available to suit different dishes. There are great advantages of cooking and serving in clay chatties. Not only do they look charming and authentic, but best of all, the flavours and aromatics build up within the clay. The more you cook the better the infusion!

CLOVES

An extremely aromatic and flavoursome dried flower bud of a variety of myrtle tree. Great for meat curries, freshly ground and in small amounts.

COCONUT

The grated coconut flesh, as well as fresh coconut milk, are used in both sweet and savoury Pacific Island dishes. The first extract of coconut is more commonly called coconut cream, whereas the second extract is the thinner coconut milk.

COCONUT CREAM

The first extraction of thick coconut milk is incredibly rich with an almost spreadable consistency.

COCONUT MILK

The second extraction of the coconut has a far thinner consistency than coconut cream. If buying tinned coconut cream or milk, always choose unsweetened varieties.

COCONUT OIL, EXTRA VIRGIN

Extra virgin (also known as full-flavoured or less refined) coconut oil is solid at room temperature. It imparts a distinctive coconut flavour to dishes. It's available from health food stores, Asian grocers and sometimes in the health food aisle of larger supermarkets.

COCONUT SCRAPER

A useful tool for grating fresh coconut. Some are free-standing, while others come with a screw-on mechanism for the tabletop.

CORIANDER ROOT

The roots of the popular coriander (cilantro) leaves have a more intense flavour and are often used in soups and curry pastes.

CURRY LEAVES

The leaves of the citrus-like tree used in Southern Indian, Sri Lankan and Malaysian cooking. Usually fried before using in curries and chutneys. Why not grow some in your herb garden at home?

CURRY POWDERS

Countless combinations of spices are used to produce an array of flavours suited to particular curries. Roasted curry powders are generally used in meat curries, have a deeper colour and more powerful flavour. Unroasted curry powder is the typical curry powder found in supermarkets. In Sri Lankan cooking it is traditionally used in vegetarian curries.

DRUMSTICK, DRUMSTICK LEAF

Drumstick is eaten like a vegetable. It is a long, ridged dark green pod. Only the soft inner pulp is used. With a somewhat bitter flavour, it is a prevailing ingredient in vegetable curries. You can also use the leaves of the plant for cooking.

FENNEL SEEDS

Roasted ground fennel seeds are a principal ingredient in Sri Lankan curry powders. Also known as sweet cumin, the flavour and aromatics resemble a more moderate and sweet aniseed.

FENUGREEK SEEDS

Small, brown, square-shaped seeds of the pea family used dried and ground in virtually all Sri Lankan curries to thicken sauces and instil a faintly bitter flavour. Use in small quantities. Be careful not to burn fenugreek, otherwise it will become bitter if overheated.

GALANGAL

Galangal is a spice used in many Indonesian dishes. It resembles ginger and has a strong peppery, slightly sour, flavour.

GHEE

A clarified butter with a pronounced flavour. It can be heated to temperatures far greater than butter without burning.

GORAKA

Also known as *gamboge*, segments of the goraka fruit, much like an orange, are dried until black. Pieces can be added to dishes whole and removed before eating or soaked in water and ground into a paste.

GOTU KOLA (PENNYWORT)

A leafy green aquatic vegetable, which is prized for its medicinal properties and health benefits. It is used throughout Asian cooking.

GROUND CORIANDER

Known to lose its flavour quite rapidly, dried coriander seeds should be freshly ground as required.

GROUND CUMIN

With a rich earthy flavour, cumin is frequently used in Sri Lankan cooking. Dried or roasted cumin seeds ground into a powder is an essential element of most spice blends.

INDIAN BLACK SALT

Also known as *kala namak*, it is sold as large rocks varying in colour from deep violet to pale rosy purple. It's available from Indian grocers.

JACKFRUIT

The outside of this fruit is prickly, much like a durian, and the inside is thick and fleshy. It can be eaten raw but when unripe its texture is similar to chicken, making it an ideal meat substitute.

KAFFIR LIME

The kaffir lime is native to Asia and both its fruit and leaves are used in many different dishes to add an aromatic citric taste.

LONGGANISA SAUSAGE

Similar to the Spanish chorizo sausage but is made with different spice blends. Each region in the Philippines has its own variation.

MACE

Mace comes from the nutmeg tree. While nutmeg is derived from the seed of the tree, mace is the hard outer shell that covers the seed. It has a more delicate flavour than nutmeg.

MALDIVE FISH FLAKES

They are Sri Lankan cuisine's equivalent to shrimp paste or fish sauce used in Thai, Indonesian or Malay cooking. Very strong in aroma and smoky flavour, they are an essential component to achieving an authentic Sri Lankan piquancy, and are added to most curries.

MANGO

This popular fruit is eaten green in salads, as well as fully ripened in many Filipino desserts, such as halo halo.

MEXICAN SPICES

This is a handy spice blend available at supermarkets in the spice aisle. It is earthy with a hint of heat.

MORTAR AND PESTLE

Usually made of stone, this duo of tools is essential for grinding fresh spices for all types of island cuisine. Freshly ground spices have a stronger and more robust flavour than pre-ground ones and make a big difference to the taste of the dish. A mortar and pestle is a good alternative to a grinding stone for creating spice pastes in your kitchen at home.

PALM OIL

Palm oil comes from the fruit of the oil palm and can be found in many Asian and Indian grocery stores.

PALM SUGAR (JAGGERY)

Palm sugar comes from the coconut flower and is used to sweeten Indonesian desserts. It gives a deep caramel flavour, similar to brown sugar.

PANDAN LEAF

Also known as *rampe* and frequently referred to as the vanilla of Asia. Pandan has long green leaves used to infuse aroma and colour into curries, rice and sweets. Pandan has a unqiue aroma and taste, there really is no substitute. It can be used as a garnish, but the leaves are not eaten and should be removed from the dish before serving.

PAPAYA

Papaya is widely grown in the Pacific Islands and is used both ripe and green, in many salads.

RICE

Rice is a staple in Indonesian cuisine and is served as an accompaniment to most dishes, sweet or savoury.

SAGO

Sago is a starch that comes from the palm and resembles small white pearls. It is commonly used to make a sweet pudding with coconut milk.

SALAM LEAVES

Salam leaves are Indonesian bay leaves. You can substitute curry leaves or bay leaves.

SALTED DUCK EGG
Duck eggs that are cured in brine. You can buy these from Chinese grocers, usually in cartons of six.

SALTPETRE
Also known as potassium nitrate, saltpetre is used to preserve sausages, bacon and gammon.

SAMBA RICE
A pungent country rice native to Sri Lanka, the grains are tiny; the powerful flavour and aroma is said to be an acquired taste.

SAMBAL
Sambal is a type of sauce made with chilli and is commonly found in many different Asian cuisines.

SEA GRAPES
Sea grapes are a type of seaweed that forms in clumps, with the appearance of a bunch of grapes.

SMOKED SEA SALT
This is essentially salt with a smoky flavour added. It can be purchased from fine food stores.

STAR FRUIT
Also known as *carambola*, this star-shaped tropical fruit has a sweet and slightly sour taste.

STRING BEANS (SITAW)
These are long, thin green beans that are a traditional accompaniment to the Filipino dish kare kare.

SURF CLAMS
These are medium-sized clams, available from good fishmongers.

TAMARIND
The brown pulp of ripe tamarind fruit has a sweet and sour flavour. The pulp is added to water and ground into a paste to be used in curries, chutneys or to tenderise meat.

TARO
The taro is a tuberous vegetable commonly used in Asian and island cuisine as an accompaniment to other dishes.

TERASI
Terasi is an Indonesian variation of shrimp paste made from fermented ground shrimp. It is widely used in Indonesian sambal.

UBE HALAYA (PURPLE YAM)
This root vegetable is bright purple in colour and is used in many Asian desserts, such as the Filipino favourite, halo halo.

TEMPERING
This is technique used in Sri Lankan and Indian cooking where you fry spices and/or curry leaves in a separate pan in oil or ghee until they are fragrant.

TURMERIC
Used in almost every curry in small quantities, adds beautiful yellow colour and is good substitute for saffron.

WATER SPINACH (KANGKUNG)
A leafy vegetable, mild in flavour. It adds a brilliant green colour to curries.

WING BEAN
These small beans with four-winged edges can be eaten pod and all when they are young. They are similar to peas in flavour.

WHITE MUSTARD SEEDS
These have a slightly milder flavour than the black mustard seeds and vary in colour from beige to pale brown.

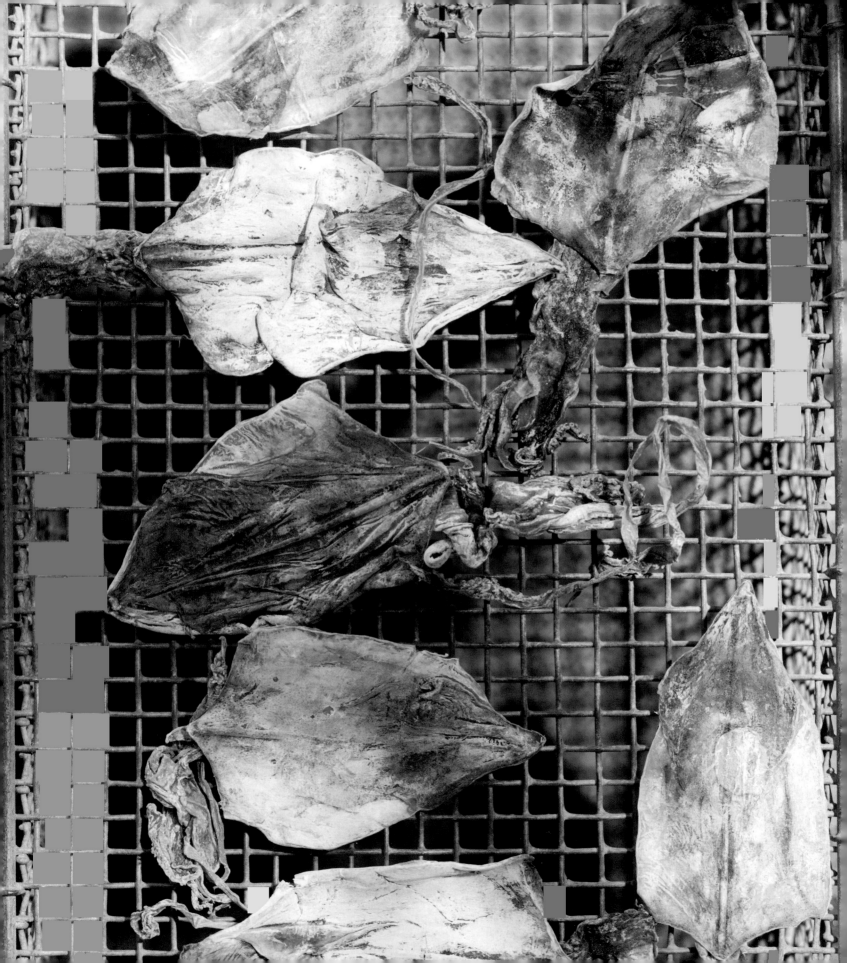

ACKNOWLEDGEMENTS

There are so many people to thank for their assistance.

Firstly to my family — although I love to travel and discover all of these amazing places and people it means I am away for up to ten weeks at a time. So to Karen, my beautiful wife, manager and organiser, thank you for your patience and all the hard work you have put in to running the Kuruvita business, as well as team Kuruvita. To team Kuruvita — my beautiful sons Jai, Marley and Taj — thank you for looking after your Mum for me while I am away, and being helpful to her.

Thank you to Erik Dwyer, Commissioning Editor of SBS, for giving me a shot and having faith in the idea, and to SBS management who have been so supportive and continue to assist and promote me, including Julianne McCormack-Brown who does an amazing job of marketing the television shows.

Thank you to Henry Motteram and Tim Whiddon from The Precinct Studios for assisting with the release of pictures and supplying me with such professional film crews while we are filming, and also to all the post-production crew that have made the show look so good.

Thank you to Gemma Kaczerepa who assisted with all the recipes for both television series.

Thank you to Dilmah tea and the founder of Dilmah, Mr Merrill J Fernando, and his sons, Dilhan and Malik, for assisting with the production of *My Sri Lanka*, and to the rest of the Dilmah team who were there to assist at any time of the day or night. We had unimpeded access to the whole of Sri Lanka and the trip to the north and east of country would not have been possible without them. Thank you to Ceylon tea for being such a pure and perfect product and an amazing ingredient to cook with.

Thank you to the people and governments of Sri Lanka, the Philippines, Indonesia, Vanuatu and the Cook Islands for welcoming us into their countries and providing us with unlimited access to all areas and permission to film. The people include: Ryan Sebastian and Venus of Philippine tourism, Papatui from Cook Island tourism, Tiri John from the Whatever Bar & Grill on Rarotonga, Cook Islands, and Shamil and the chefs assistants in Sri Lanka.

Thank you to my cook's assistant for *Island Feast*, Regan Kelly, who through a lot of adverse events assisted me to source and produce the food for the show.

Back at home, I'd like to thank for this book: Paul McNally and Hannah Koelmeyer from Hardie Grant Books; Michelle Noerianto, the best food stylist in the world; Peta Dent, food tester extraordinare, who worked with me during the photo shoot; Chris Chen, who took all the beautiful food shots; Emilia Toia, the art director and designer, and Belinda So for her words and editing.

To all of you, thank you so much. It is your passion and professionalism that has made this book what it is.

Peter Kuruvita

An SBS book

Published in 2012 by Hardie Grant Books

Hardie Grant Books (Australia)
Ground Floor, Building 1
658 Church Street
Richmond, Victoria 3121
www.hardiegrant.com.au

Hardie Grant Books (UK)
Dudley House, North Suite
34–35 Southampton Street
London WC2E 7HF
www.hardiegrant.co.uk

A Cataloguing-in-Publication entry is available from the
catalogue of the National Library of Australia at www.nla.gov.au

My Feast, with Peter Kuruvita
ISBN 9781742705118

Publishing director: Paul McNally
Project editor: Hannah Koelmeyer
Editor: Bel So
Design manager: Heather Menzies
Design and art direction: Emilia Toia
Photographer: Chris Chen
Stylist: Michelle Noerianto
Production manager: Todd Rechner
Production assistant: Sarah Trotter

Colour reproduction by Splitting Image Colour Studio
Printed in China by 1010 Printing International Limited